AIDS TO THE PSALMS

Exploring The Message, Cycle A

BY HUGH H. DRENNAN

C.S.S. Publishing Co., Inc.
Lima, Ohio

AIDS TO THE PSALMS

Copyright © 1992 by
The C.S.S. Publishing Company, Inc.
Lima, Ohio

All rights reserved. No part of this publication may be reproduced, stored in a retrieval system, or transmitted in any form or by any means, electronic, mechanical, photocopying, recording, or otherwise, without the prior permission of the publisher. Inquiries should be addressed to: The C.S.S. Publishing Company, Inc., 628 South Main Street, Lima, Ohio 45804.

Scripture quotations are from the New Revised Standard Version of the Bible, copyright 1989 by the Division of Christian Education of the National Council of the Churches of Christ in the USA. Used by permission.

Library of Congress Cataloging-in-Publication Data
(Revised for volume 2)

Drennan, Hugh H., 1942
  Aids to the Psalms.
  Cover subtitle: Exploring the message.
  Contents: [1] Cycle C
  1. Bible. O.T. Psalms — Criticism, interpretation, etc., I. Title.
  BS1430.2.d68   1991   264'.34   91-22755
  ISBN 1-55673-345-3 (Cycle C)
  ISBN 1-55673-435-2 (Cycle A)

9238 / ISBN 1-55673-435-2   PRINTED IN U.S.A.

Dedication

This book is dedicated to the Rev. W. Richard McEuen who early on shared with me his wonderful vision of a sovereign God who cares passionately and providentially for all creation. It is my hope that this book reflects that same perspective.

Preface

This series of books grew out of a need for a daily spiritual discipline. After experimenting with several forms of writing I decided on reflections upon the Psalms in the form you now see them. This discipline has greatly enriched my understanding of the Psalms and depth of feeling they reflect for common human experiences. I believe all of us can identify and benefit from the wisdom contained in these ageless songs of life.

The reader should be able to use this volume in many ways. The messages can be used for daily meditations and devotions. Since they are based upon the lectionary readings, pastors may find they are helpful in priming the pump for sermons. Pastors and worship leaders may also find them helpful in liturgical settings. Educators may find them helpful for a study of the Psalms. They may also be helpful for those times when we are called upon to provide a mediation at the beginning or close of a meeting or fellowship opportunity. I am certain there are many other uses the reader will be able to discern.

It is my hope that the words of this volume will stimulate your imagination and help open the door for the Holy Spirit to touch you as you continue your own spiritual journey.

Psalm Selections For Year A

Sunday	Psalm	Page
Advent 1	122	13
Advent 2	72:1-8	15
Advent 3	146:5-10	17
Advent 4	24	19
Christmas Eve Day	96	21
Christmas Day	97	23
Christmas 1	111	25
New Year's	67	27
Christmas 2	147:12-20	29
Epiphany	72:1-14	31
Baptism of Jesus	29	33
Epiphany 2	40:1-11	35
Epiphany 3	27:1-6	37
Epiphany 4	37:1-11	39
Epiphany 5	112:4-9	41
Epiphany 6	119:1-8	43
Epiphany 7	62:5-12	45
Epiphany 8	119:33-40	47
Last Sunday After Epiphany	2:6-11	49
Ash Wednesday	51:1-12	51
Lent 1	130	53
Lent 2	33:18-22	55
Lent 3	95	57
Lent 4	23	59
Lent 5	116:1-9	61
Lent 6 (Passion)	31:9-16	63
Palm Sunday	118:19-29	65

Sunday	Psalm	Page
Holy Week		
Monday	36:5-10	67
Tuesday	71:1-12	69
Wednesday	70	71
Maundy Thursday	89:20-21, 24, 26	73
Good Friday	22:1-18	75
Easter	118:14-24	77
Easter Evening	150	79
Easter 2	16:5-11	81
Easter 3	116:12-19	83
Easter 4	23	85
Easter 5	31:1-8	87
Easter 6	66:8-20	89
Ascension Sunday	47	91
Easter 7	68:1-10	93
Pentecost	104:24-34	95
Trinity	33:1-12	97
Proper 4	33:12-22	99
Proper 5	13	101
Proper 6	46	103
Proper 7	91:1-10	105
Proper 8	17:1-7, 15	107
Proper 9	124	109
Proper 10	69:6-15	111
Proper 11	103:1-13	113
Proper 12	105:1-11	115
Proper 13	143:1-10	117
Proper 14	106:4-12	119
Proper 15	78:1-3, 10-20	121

Sunday	Psalm	Page
Proper 16	95	123
Proper 17	114	125
Proper 18	115:1-11	127
Proper 19	19:7-14	129
Proper 20	106:7-8, 19-23	131
Proper 21	99	133
Proper 22	81:1-10	135
Proper 23	135:1-14	137
Proper 24	146	139
Proper 25	128	141
Proper 26	127	143
Proper 27	50:7-15	145
Proper 28	76	147
Proper 29	23	149
Thanksgiving	65	151

Key Words In Understanding the Psalms

There are many words that help us better understand the Psalms. Following is a short list of words that may help the reader to peer more deeply into the words of the psalmist.

Psalm. The word psalm simply means song. It does not infer any particular religious tone; psalms can be secular or sacred. Yet, in our book of Psalms they are very religious. The psalmist may be happy with God and the world, unhappy or angry with God and life, but the psalms of the Bible are always directed toward God; that makes them religious.

Torah. Torah means teaching. This is lively teaching which includes the concept of revelation. In this type of teaching the mind and purpose of God is revealed. The students in turn are the people of God.

Yahweh. Yahweh was regarded as God's personal name. This name was so holy it could not be spoken. When the Hebrews were reading Scripture and encountered this word, they would say Lord instead.

Covenant. Covenant is at the Heart of Judaism. Covenant represents the special relationship, agreement between God and a selected or called people. Covenant is different than contract in that it is God who sets the terms and calls both parties to live up to that agreement.

Hesed. Hesed stands at the heart of God's covenant. It is a difficult word to translate; the writers of the King James Version of the Bible used 45 different words to translate it: mercy, goodness, love, loving-kindness . . . Now we understand hesed as God's gracious love and loyalty through which God connects himself to Israel through the covenant.

Other Terms Of The Covenant

The Hebrew language is gender directed. Some words are masculine and some feminine. Understanding this helps the reader to see the richness of the passages. For example, concepts of the sky, what is above, is usually masculine in gender. Words connected with the earth below are usually feminine in gender. For example, God is masculine and earth is feminine. The words of salvation, *yesha* is masculine and represents what God has done for us. On the other hand, *yeshu'ah*, a feminine word, is what empowers us to communicate God's saving love to others. *Tsedeq* is a masculine word about God's righteousness and *tsedaqah* is a feminine word for righteousness relating to human responses to God's righteousness. Mercy comes from a Hebrew word for womb; it is a type of overpowering love that mothers have for their children, the issue of their womb. This is the divine mother concept in Hebraic thought. In mercy God forgives us even before we ask to be forgiven. There are many psalms of this nature which are grateful for what God has already done for us. Finally, there is a word often translated as soul, *Nephesh*. This word has been corrupted by Greek thought which separated body, mind and soul. All three of these entities are included in the Hebrew concept of soul. The idea of saving soul or the immortality of the soul is foreign to early Hebrew thought. Soul refers to one total being and how our total being relates to all other parts of creation. Soul is our basic personality derived from both heredity and environment.

Advent 1

Psalm 122

I was glad when they said to me,
   "Let us go to the house of the Lord!"
Our feet are standing
   within your gates,
      O Jerusalem.
Jerusalem — built as a city
   that is bound firmly together.
To it the tribes go up,
   the tribes of the Lord,
as was decreed for Israel,
   to give thanks to the name of the Lord.
For there the thrones for judgment were set up,
the thrones of the house of David.
Pray for the peace of Jerusalem:
   "May they prosper who love you.
Peace be within your walls,
   and security within your towers."
For the sake of my relatives and friends
   I will say, "Peace be within you."
For the sake of the house of the Lord our God,
   I will seek your good.

Alternate Image

   The Singer has undergone a long, long pilgrimage. Throughout her journey she has carried, dragged and pulled a large gunny sack. Now, at last, she stands at the gate of the city of peace, her destination. Dragging her gunny sack, she joins a processional with other sack draggers toward an enormous hole in the ground. She stands at the edge of the abyss and peers down into sheer nothingness. She reaches into her gunny sack and pulls out a huge rock of avarice and throws it into the pit. Relieved, her back straightens and she feels better. She reaches for another rock. It is a rock of greed. She tosses it into the pit. She straightens more and feels renewed. She gathers and tosses more rocks from her gunny sack — rocks of jealousy, anger and self-righteousness. Rock after rock is heaved into the pit. She feels better, stronger and more whole with the toss of each rock. Finally, she rolls a huge boulder of pride into the pit and as she watches it disappear she feels a great sensation of peace. She notices that each time she throws a rock from her gunny sack into the pit the backs of those around her also straighten. As they throw their own rocks into the pit, she feels better as well. She joins hands with her fellow rock-throwers and they dance and sing with a joy she had forgotten. It is good to be there. Truly, this is a city of peace: a Jeru-Shalom.

Reflection

Jerusalem means city or foundation of peace. Jerusalem was more than a city or a capital. It represented a place of peace and justice. On our spiritual journeys we seek that peace that passes all understanding. We seek a peace that brings a sense of well-being into our lives, a peace that makes us whole. But so often on our journeys, instead of feeling better, we just pick up more stones, more weight, more sin, more guilt and move farther from a sense of peace. Then, God marvelously focuses our eyes upon our elder brother Jesus. He has walked the road for us. He gladly takes our bags of sins from us and tosses them into the abyss where they are totally and completely destroyed. Jesus offers us health, wellness, spirituality and peace. It is good for us to seek the house of the Lord and offer our burdens to the Master of the house. The Master will take our burdens and replace them with the peace that passes all understanding.

Advent 2

Psalm 72:1-8

Give the king your justice, O God,
 and your righteousness to a king's son.
May he judge your people with righteousness,
 and your poor with justice.
May the mountains yield prosperity for the people,
 and the hills, in righteousness.
May he defend the cause of the poor to the people,
 give deliverance to the needs,
 and crush the oppressor.
May he live while the sun endures,
 and as long as the mooon, throughout all generations.
May he be like rain that falls on the mown grass,
 like showers that water the earth.
In his days may righteousness flourish
 and peace abound, until the moon is no more.

Alternate Image

The Singer ambles down the road kicking an occasional stone, plucking a random strand of grass to suck on or wiggling his toes in the dirt. Carefree and aimless, the Singer wanders along the road. Suddenly the Singer is accosted by two women arguing vehemently. Unable to settle their differences, they charge him to settle their squabble. Nonplussed, the Singer pauses, listens to their arguments and then makes what he hopes is a just decision. The women grumble, but thank him for his involvement. The Singer continues down the road but before he can regain his ease, two men stop him and ask him to settle their argument. Once more the Singer listens to their viewpoints and then renders his verdict that he considers equitable. Before he can continue a rod down the road, more folk clamor around him demanding that he arbitrate their disputes. From early morning till after sundown the Singer listens, considers and renders judgments. Sometimes folk agree with his opinions, sometimes not, but order appears to reign in the village. In the days that follow, the Singer becomes the local magistrate. He continues to administer justice and assume responsibility for the order of the village. He no longer wanders down the road aimlessly. He wonders, "How did this happen?"

Reflection

God has been and always will be concerned with social justice. God wants justice and order to govern human lives on earth. God calls people to ensure that justice takes place. The Hebrew word for justice in this passage is plural. It is something we miss in English translations. God requires justice. We cannot do one act of justice and then continue merrily on our way. We must continually act justly and create order. This is what God calls each of us to do. When we accept these responsibilities our communities enjoy a state of well-being and are rich. They are rich in fellowship with each other and with the land.

Advent 3

Psalm 146:5-10

Happy are those whose help is the God of Jacob,
    whose hope is in the Lord their God,
who made heaven and earth,
    the sea, and all that is in them;
who keep faith forever;
    who executes justice for the oppressed;
who gives food to the hungry.
The Lord sets the prisoners free;
    the Lord opens the eyes of the blind.
The Lord lifts up those who are bowed down;
    the Lord loves the righteous.
The Lord watches over the strangers;
    he upholds the orphan and the widow,
but the way of the wicked he brings to ruin.
The Lord will reign forever,
    your God, O Zion, for all generations.
Praise the Lord!

Alternate Image

    The Singer is at the track betting on a horse; a sure thing she has been told. The horse loses. Returning home ready to confess her sins to her husband, she finds a note saying her husband has left her for an older woman. She drives to her parents for solace and finds an ambulance taking her father and mother away; both suffered heart attacks while making love. She calls her church and finds that her pastor is away at a conference on handling grief. She listens to the radio on her drive home and hears that the president of the country resigned from office after being discovered in a clandestine intrigue with the Pope. The Singer pulls to the side of the road, turns off the car motor and sighs, "Who can you trust?" She closes her eyes in prayer. After a moment she opens her eyes and turns the key in the ignition; it works. The sun streams in the car window and bathes her in relaxing warmth. A quick cloud-burst washes away the dirt from her car and brings a fresh smell to the earth. At home, her children hug her and cradle her head upon their shoulders. Inside her home, they laugh at her foolish escapade at the race track. They lament her husband's absence without malice. They ready themselves to go to the hospital and burst into laughter about the cause of her parents' illnesses. On their way to the hospital a radio commentator updates the news about the president and the Pope. Their clandestine endeavor was to create a promising new peace plan they are presenting to the United Nations. The Singer offers her prayer of thanks and praises to God, the source of her trust.

Reflection

It is very easy for us to be disillusioned in this world because, so often, we put our trust in that which is untrustworthy. Even those with good intent cannot offer eternal help. The parents who tell their child that they will be with them always because they love them mislead their children and promote mistrust. God, not we, determines the length of relationships here and beyond. God is to be the source of our trust. God, and God only, will reign forever. Trust in God enables trust in the rest of life.

Advent 4

Psalm 24

The earth is the Lord's and all that is in it,
 the world, and those who live in it;
for he has founded it on the seas,
 and established it on the rivers.
Who shall ascend the hill of the Lord?
 And who shall stand in his holy place?
Those who have clean hands and pure hearts.
 who do not lift up their souls to what is false,
 and do not swear deceitfully.
They will receive blessing from the Lord,
 and vindication from the God of their salvation.
Such is the company of those who seek him,
 who seek the face of the God of Jacob.
Lift up your heads, O gates!
 and be lifted up, O ancient doors!
 that the King of glory may come in.
Who is the King of glory?
 The Lord, strong and mighty,
 The Lord, mighty in battle.
Lift up your heads, O gates!
 and be lifted up, O ancient doors!
 that the King of glory may come in.
Who is this King of glory?
 the Lord of hosts,
 he is the King of glory.

Alternate Image

 The Singer is preparing to go to church. He lays out his suit, a new shirt and tie, fresh socks and underwear. He brushes his teeth and then steps into the shower. He happily shampoos his hair and scrubs his body while singing a hymn. He examines his hands — they are still quite dirty. He grabs a strong pumice soap and lathers his hands vigorously, but when he rinses away the suds, his hands are still dirty. He tries detergent after detergent to no avail; his hands just will not come clean. Dejected, he steps out of the shower, towels himself dry and puts on his new clothes, but they do not bring joy in the wearing. The Singer slowly walks to the church, climbs the steps to the sanctuary and is stopped by the head usher. The usher eyes him and then challenges, "Have you kept the 10 commandments? Have you fulfilled the teachings of Jesus? Are your hands clean?" Hiding his hands behind his pockets, the Singer mumbles, "No." "Then why are you here?" demands the usher. "I want to worship the Lord my God," the Singer responds meekly. "Okay," says the usher and escorts the Singer into the sanctuary. At a pew the usher smiles and holds out his hand to shake the hand of the Singer. Timidly the Singer offers his hands as well. Then, in amazement, the Singer sees that his hands are clean.

Reflection

This psalm lifts up the essential need we have to worship God. For life to have meaning and value, it must have a worthy center, God. It is in worship that we acknowledge that center and feel the wholeness we are intended to have. We also need to prepare ourselves to worship. Sometimes we try to make ourselves worthy to worship; that does not work. No matter how hard we try to follow the law, the teachings of Jesus, we always come up short. No one deserves to go to the Lord's house. Fortunately, worthiness is not what is required. What is required is the desire to worship. We need to acknowledge the need to focus our lives on God. What is important is our intent. When God prompts that intention in our lives and we respond appropriately, then God moves to make us worthy to be in the Lord's house. Jesus once again washes our hands and feet and makes us welcome.

Christmas Eve

Psalm 96

O Sing to the Lord a new song;
    sing to the Lord, all the earth.
Sing to the Lord, bless his name;
    tell of his salvation from day to day.
Declare his glory among the nations,
    his marvelous works among all the peoples.
For great is the Lord, and greatly to be praised;
    he is to be revered above all gods.
For all the gods of the peoples are idols,
    but the Lord made the heavens.
Honor and majesty are before him;
    strength and beauty are in his sanctuary.
Ascribe to the Lord, O families of the peoples,
    ascribe to the Lord glory and strength.
Ascribe to the Lord the glory due his name;
    bring an offering, and come into his courts.
Worship the Lord in holy splendor;
    tremble before him, all the earth.

Alternate Image

   The Singer is in the sanctuary planting seeds. She has made flower boxes and spread them all around the sanctuary; on window ledges, in the choir loft, on the organ, and at the ends of the pews. Some boxes hang from the rafters, some line the aisles, all are orderly and neat. Now she is planting seeds in them. Some seeds will mature quickly and some slowly. She plans the planting so that there will be new flowers and plants each Sunday worshipers come to praise God. The Singer plants a myriad of flowers from simple pansies to rare orchids. She also plants seeds of produce: cotton seeds, corn seeds, bean seeds, wheat seeds, tree seeds, bush seeds — seeds that can remind the worshipers of God's creative abundance and nurture of the people. In the pews the Singer plants new seeds — seeds of justice, seeds of peace, seeds of equity, seeds of righteousness and seeds of love. The Singer plants the last seed and stands back to view her work. She is confident that the seeds will receive the warmth of the Son, will flourish from the melodious hymn notes dropping as gentle rain from the rafters, and be cultivated by caring disciples. She is confident of the harvest God will bring from her planting.

Reflection

God is the God of newness. God continually creates new things. Newness in nature. Newness in plant and animal life. Newness and order from chaos. God is the God of Genesis, of beginnings. God is the God of David, a shepherd. God is the God of the vineyard. God is the God of the plain. God is the God of all creation. God is the father of Jesus, the re-creator. Each day we are new as well, regenerated through sleep and fast-breaking. Each day offers us new opportunities to sing God praises. Each moment brings us fresh ideas and openings for service. We can use all these to sing songs of praise to our God.

Christmas Day

Psalm 97

The Lord is King! Let the earth rejoice:
  let the many coastlands be glad!
Clouds and thick darkness are all around him;
  righteousness and justice are the foundation of his throng.
Fire goes before him,
  and consumes his adversaries on every side.
His lightnings light up the world;
  the earth sees and trembles.
The mountains melt like wax before the Lord,
  before the Lord of all the earth.
The heavens proclaim his righteousness;
  and all the peoples behold his glory.
All worshipers of images are put to shame,
  those who make their boast in worthless idols;
  all gods bow down before him.
Zion hears and is glad and the towns of Judah rejoice,
  because of your judgments, O God.
For you, O Lord, are most high over all the earth;
  you are exalted far above all gods.
The Lord loves those who hate evil; he guards the lives of his
      faithful;
  he rescues them from the hand of the wicked.
Light dawns for the righteous,
  and joy for the upright in heart.
Rejoice in the Lord, O you righteous,
  and give thanks to his holy name!

Alternate Image

  The Singer tightly grips the armrests of his airplane seat. The turbos roar, the plan accelerates down the runway, the

Singer grips ever more tightly. The plane tilts upward, lifts off the runway and the Singer's heart pounds and rises to his throat. The plane bounces on stormy thermal columns and the Singer's head wags from side to side. The storm's rain pelts the plane's fuselage as sweat forms on the Singer's brow. The Singer compares the rocky ride of the plane through the storm with the rocky journey of his life. Perils loom at every juncture, threatening the Singer. The Singer momentarily closes his eyes in prayer. As his eyes blink open the plane emerges above the clouds. Brilliant sunlight bathes the soft clouds in beautiful luminescence. It is beautiful. It is serene. It is calm. The beauty of God's creation, hidden in the storm, bursts forth in magnificent splendor. Bathed in the glory of God's creation the Singer relaxes, secure and confident and the plane wings onward to its destination.

Reflection

God often appears hidden to us. It is hidden because we look in the wrong places or for the wrong things. We place shaky confidence in the images and idols of modern life and then quake in the tempests of our life. The more caught up in our pandemonium of our lives the more chaotic our lives become. Then God breaks through our cloudy vision and grants us peace. Peace that comes with the realization that God is indeed in control of the universe and all is well. When we relinquish our frenzied desire to control events and seek God's will, respite floods into our being and faith brightens our horizons. Lifted by God's grace above the storms, we with God cast aside evil and work for righteousness. And we rejoice in God's providence.

Christmas 1

Psalm 111

Praise the Lord!
I will give thanks to the Lord with my whole heart,
    in the company of the upright, in the congregation.
Great are the works of the Lord,
    studied by all who delight in them.
Full of honor and majesty is his work,
    and his righteousness endures forever.
He has gained renown by his wonderful deeds;
    the Lord is gracious and merciful.
He provides food for those who fear him;
    he is ever mindful of his covenant.
He has shown his people the power of his works,
    in giving them the heritage of the nations.
The works in his hands are faithful and just;
    all his precepts are trustworthy.
They are established forever and ever,
    to be performed with faithfulness and uprightness.
He sent redemption to his people;
    he has commanded his covenant forever.
    Holy and awesome is his name.
The fear of the Lord is the beginning of wisdom;
    all those who practice it have a good understanding.
    His praise endures forever.

Alternate Image

The Singer tends her garden. She painstakingly prepares a good seedbed. She plants the seeds carefully at the proper depth. She spreads fertilizer evenly and in the correct proportions. She waters the garden and waits expectantly for the seeds to grow. No seeds sprout, none at all. The only growth that takes place is ugly weeds. The Singer cultivates the rows, pulling the offending weeds from the garden and waits for the seeds to sprout. The seeds stay dormant, but the weeds return worse than before. She waters the garden and the ground cracks as though parched. She drains standing water and the garden turns into a swamp. Her garden makes no horticultural sense. Why does it not respond to her care? Nature appears turned upside down. She screams her complaint, her charge of injustice to God. God arrives. God asks the Singer, "Did we make an agreement about your garden? Did I agree with you to make orderly the workings of nature? Did I promise to grow the seeds you planted? Did I covenant with you to create the miracles of land to produce crops?" The Singer acknowledges that she has not made such a covenant with God and stands dejected in the barren land. God turns to her and says, "No. But I have made just a covenant." As God leaves, the Singer turns to watch and sees the garden blossom in abundance.

Reflection

How easily it is for us to take the blessings of nature for granted. We spend far more time complaining about the weather than we do in thanking God for the seasons. We are more inclined to grumble about the limits of the harvest than we are to thank God for the miracle of growing things. We are more likely to crab about the little annoyances in our lives than we are to stand in awe of the wonders of creation. But God has made a covenant with us and blessed us even in our complaints and our faithlessness. God sends the bounty of nature to all people. God expresses his love through nature. God made that love obvious by coming to us as a babe in the manger to redeem the world. How wonderful it is when we look up from our petty complaints and see the majesty and love of God all about us. Then we begin to see clearly and taste wisdom.

New Year's Day

Psalm 67

May God be gracious to us and bless us
and make his face to shine upon us,
that your way may be known upon the earth,
your saving power among all nations.
Let the peoples praise you, O God;
let all the peoples praise you.
Let the nations be glad and sing for joy,
for you judge the peoples with equity
and guide the nations upon earth.
Let the peoples praise you, O God;
let all the peoples praise you.
The earth has yielded its increase.
May God continue to bless us;
let all the ends of the earth revere him.

Alternate Image

The Singer received God's blessing of wisdom. The Singer took that blessing he cherished and went into a cave to use that blessing of wisdom to understand the world in quiet and solitude. In the darkness of the cave the Singer recalled the light of the world that illuminated God's creation. The Singer pondered the relationship between earth, sea and air in God's creation. The Singer wrote volume after volume of his discernments about the world and stacked them in a corner of the cave to read again later. The Singer worked all his life in the cave attempting to use God's blessing of wisdom to understand the world better. But, as time went on, the Singer noticed that it became ever harder to discern truth. And as his life drew to a close he realized that he had never shared one piece of his wisdom with another person. As he died, he said, "This was a mistake." Perhaps his one truly wise understanding.

The Singer received God's blessing of wisdom. The Singer took his blessing throughout his journey on the face of God's good earth. He readily shared his insights with others on their journeys and listened to their shared wisdom, which in turn increased his own. Sometimes he withdrew from the crowds to contemplate more fully the truths he discovered. But always he would return to the road to share his new insights with others and gain their opinions. As life went on, the blessing of wisdom increased and the insight came ever more rapidly. Near the end of his life the Singer reflected on the conversations he had shared, the books he had written, the interaction of wisdom in the lives he had contacted. He would carry on truths he had learned.

Reflection

God's blessings are tangible. They are like sunlight shining upon our faces. Better yet God's blessings shine with us as we walk spiritual journeys. The blessings are so great they should never be limited solely to the one who received them. The blessing are to be shared, so that through us, God blesses others. We become vehicles of God's blessings. Thus, blessings and we have a purpose. We are God's agents in this world so that all people may know of God's all pervasive love. Bounty is to be shared.

Christmas 2

Psalm 147:12-20

Praise the Lord, O Jerusalem!
    Praise your God, O Zion!
For he strengthens the bars of your gates;
    he blesses your children within you.
He grants peace within your borders;
    he fills you with the finest of wheat.
He sends out his command to the earth;
    his word runs swiftly.
He gives snow like wool;
    he scatters frost like ashes.
He hurls down hail like crumbs —
    who can stand before his cold?
He sends out his word, and melts them;
    he makes his wind blow, and the waters flow.
He declares his word to Jacob,
    his statutes and ordinances to Israel.
He has not dealt thus with any other nation;
    they do not know his ordinances.
Praise the Lord!

Alternate Image

    The Singer returns home for Christmas. She attends a Christmas Eve service in the church of her childhood. She finds that church, strong, happy, peaceful and faithful. The children's voices create a gentle breeze of happy notes that tumble delightfully around the congregation's ears. The words of the nativity the lector reads irrigate the minds of the worshipers with God's cleansing word of hope and joy. The spirit of revelation invades each mind with new truth perceptions as the pastor proclaims the word to that time and place. Life's confusion is sloughed off as the simple message of God's love personified in the gift of a child, God's child, permeates the minds and hearts of those gathered. The Singer wonders, "Why are these people so blessed? Are they more intelligent, more gifted than others? Are they more discerning, more servant directed, more faithful in their discipleship than others? Why is this church so strong, happy, peaceful and faithful?" Then the babe's voice echoes in her mind, "Because I love them!" The Singer's eyes brighten, calm and well-being infest every pore of her body, and synapse of her brain, every portion of her soul. Feeling loved, the Singer adds her voice to the congregation's and sings, "Praise the Lord!"

Reflection

Life is so complicated today. Voices surround us on every side, giving us conflicting advice and contradictory priorities. "Build financial security through a strong stock portfolio." "Use our cosmetics and stay forever young; the world belongs to the youth." "Protect our freedom, join the armed forces." "You are what you eat." "Be confident, use deodorant." "Clothes make the man." "Cross your heart." "Do." "Don't." Sometimes it is very appropriate to return to your childhood when life was less complex. A time of simple, yet profound truths. But how can we do that? How can we find our way to simple truths, clear insight and strong faith? We can't. But God can. The blessings of peace, the certainty of faith, the strength of belief are gifts bestowed upon us by a God who loves us with infinite compassion. Enjoy the gift of these blessings and add your praise to the choir of believers.

Epiphany

Psalm 72:1-14

Give the king your justice, O God,
  and your righteousness to a king's son.
May he judge your people with righteousness,
  and your poor with justice.
May the mountains yield prosperity for the people,
  and the hills, in righteousness.
May he defend the cause of the poor of the people,
  give deliverance to the needy,
  and crush the oppressor.
May he live while the sun endures,
  and as long as the moon, throughout all generations.
May he be like rain that falls on the mown grass,
  like showers that water the earth.
In his days may righteousness flourish
  and peace abound, until the moon is no more.
May he have dominion from sea to sea,
  and from the River to the ends of the earth.
May his foes bow down before him,
  and his enemies lick the dust.
May the kings of Tarshish and of the isles
  render him tribute,
may the kings of Sheba and Seba bring gifts.
May all kings fall down before him,
  all nations give him service.
For he delivers the needy when they call,
  the poor and those who have no helper.
He has pity on the weak and the needy,
  and saves the lives of the needy.
From oppression and violence he redeems their life;
  and precious is their blood in his sight.

Alternate Image

The Singer does not feel well. His feet hurt, his back is sore, his head aches, his muscles are stiff, his bones arthritic. How did he get into such miserable shape? The Singer acknowledges that most of his aches and pains are the result of his not caring for his body, not giving it proper exercise and diet and not giving it the attention it deserves. The Singer resolves to embark upon a care program for his body, and that he will begin that program today. The Singer leaves his house and takes clothing and food to a drop-in center. While there he cooks food and visits with the homeless. His feet feel better. Next, the Singer takes his bottles and cans to a recycling center. His muscles loosen. The Singer visits a prison and shares his thoughts with a discussion group. His back relaxes and he stands straighter. The Singer intervenes in a fight on a playground, soothing troubled brows and giving an attentive ear. His bones straighten. The Singer shares his ideas on a church committee on peacemaking. His head is freed of its ache. At the end of the day, the Singer is amazed at his sense of well-being. He feels quite prosperous.

Reflection

We often translate the Hebrew word *Shalom* as peace. Shalom is a richer word than that. It has to do with a sense of great well-being; a total sense of health. Directly tied to our well-being is everyone's well-being. Justice, equity, righteousness lifted up in this Psalm attest to that well-being. True well-being cannot exist solely through individual piety. For us to be truly well, all of society and all creation must be healthy as well. We cannot be a prosperous people when some of us live in poverty. To gain physical well-being, we know we have to exercise, eat properly and care for our bodies. The same is true for our spiritual well-being. We need to exercise our concern for others and in doing so we become in tune with God's will and God's peace. Well-being may flood through our lives.

Baptism Of Jesus

Psalm 29

Ascribe to the Lord, O heavenly beings,
  ascribe to the Lord glory and strength.
Ascribe to the Lord the glory of his name;
  worship the Lord in holy splendor.
The voice of the Lord is over the waters;
  the God of glory thunders,
  the Lord, over mighty waters.
The voice of the Lord is powerful;
  the voice of the Lord is full of majesty.
The voice of the Lord breaks the cedars;
  the Lord breaks the cedars of Lebanon.
He makes Lebanon skip like a calf,
  and Sirion like a young wild ox.
The voice of the Lord flashes
  forth flames of fire.
The voice of the Lord shakes the wilderness;
  the Lord shakes the wilderness of Kadesh.
The voice of the Lord causes the oaks to whirl,
  and strips the forest bare;
  and in his temple all say, "Glory!"
The Lord sits enthroned over the flood;
  the Lord sits enthroned as king forever.
May the Lord give strength to his people!
  May the Lord bless his people with peace!

Alternate Image

    The Singer is taking a nature walk. She walks beside a silvery stream brimming with fresh, clean burbling water. The Singer says, "Bless you little brook, rushing so hurriedly along." The brook streams along its way. The Singer spys a shiny round rock beside the creek. She picks it up, admires and caresses its smoothness and says, "Bless you little stone for your strong, round toughness." She sets the rock down and it sits once again by the stream. Suddenly a cloudburst soaks the Singer with its rain. The Singer says, "Bless you, oh gentle rain, for refreshing the earth." The rain falls awhile and then stops. The Singer stops to rest under the shade of a large oak tree. As she relaxes, she says, "Bless you, great shade tree, for providing a place of respite and a roosting place for the birds." The tree just stands there. In her reverie beneath the tree, the Singer considers that neither stream, rock, rain, nor tree acknowledged or responded to her blessing and acknowledgment of their importance. A smile crosses the Singer's face as she lays down on the grass beneath the tree and says, "Bless you, God, for all the blessings of nature that enrich our lives." And there, on a whisper on the wind, the Singer hears, "Thank you."

Reflection

It is good to be thankful for the gifts of creation. It is good to number and acknowledge them. But more importantly we need to offer our thanks and praise to the one who created nature. It is good to feel kinship with nature, to talk about mother earth, sister sky, brother wolf and cousin grain. Those are imaginative ways of understanding that we are all parts of God's creation and that we bear responsibility for our nature family. However, we need to be clear who is the creator and what is the created and give thanks appropriately.

Epiphany 2

Psalm 40:1-11

I waited patiently for the Lord;
   he inclined to me and heard by cry.
He drew me up from the desolate pit,
   out of the miry bog,
and set my feet upon a rock,
   making my steps secure.
He put a new song in my mouth,
   a song of praise to our God.
Many will see and fear,
   and put their trust in the Lord.
Happy are those who make
   the Lord their trust,
who do not turn to the proud,
   to those who go astray after false gods.
You have multiplied, O Lord my God,
   your wondrous deeds and your thoughts toward us;
   none can compare with you.
Were I to proclaim and tell of them,
   they would be more than can be counted.
Sacrifice and offering you do not desire.
   but you have given me an open ear.
Burnt offering and sin offering
   you have not required.
Then I said, "Here I am;
   in the scroll of the book it is written of me.
I delight to do your will, O my God;
   your law is within my heart."
I have told the glad news of deliverance
   in the great congregation;
see, I have not restrained my lips,
   as you know, O Lord.

I have not hidden your saving help within my heart,
I have spoken of your faithfulness and your salvation;
I have not concealed your steadfast love and your faithfulness from the congregation.
Do not, O Lord, withhold your mercy from me;
let your steadfast love and your faithfulness keep me safe forever.

Alternate Image

The Singer sits, waiting to be released from the detox center. The Singer considers all that he has done to his body. Booze and drugs were the gods of his life for so long and they still beckon seductively. The Singer's eye catches sight of his new friend, a minister. Here was the one who sat and held him through the hell of withdrawal. The minister offers him his blessing, the blessing of one who trusts God's reality over hazy drug perceptions. The Singer receives these blessings, puts his hand in the hand of the minister and pulls away from the pit.

Reflection

There are many pits in our lives. Thousands of hands in those pits are reaching out to grab at our feet and hands, our heads and hearts, to drag us down to the befuddlement of lesser realities. Their offer is like that of the work of pain killers. Pain tells us what is wrong with us. God does not want us to just be numb and ignore the pain of living, but to learn from life's pain and to turn to God for eventual eradication of that pain. Sin, our ultimate pain, is important. When we turn to God and offer God our sins, they are erased and we may sing our new songs.

Epiphany 3

Psalm 27:1-6

The Lord is my light and my salvation;
   whom shall I fear?
The Lord is the stronghold of my life;
   of whom shall I be afraid?
When evildoers assail me
   to devour my flesh —
my adversaries and foes —
   they shall stumble and fall.
Though an army encamp against me,
   my heart shall not fear;
though war rise up against me,
   yet I will be confident.
One thing I asked of the Lord,
   that will I seek after:
to live in the house of the Lord
   all the days of my life,
to behold the beauty of the Lord,
   and to inquire in his temple.
For he will hide me in his shelter
   in the day of trouble;
he will conceal me under the cover of his tent;
   he will set me high on a rock.
Now my head is lifted up
   above my enemies all around me,
and I will offer in his tent
   sacrifices with shouts of joy;
I will sing and make melody to the Lord.

Alternate Image

   The Singer begins to walk on a wire stretched tightly between the banks of a raging river. As he begins, a bird swoops past his ear diving for a fish it spied in the river. The Singer continues steadily walking. A few steps later a bullet whizzes past his ear and the report of a rifle echoes up and down the river canyon; a hunter has taken a shot at the bird, nearly hitting the Singer. The Singer continues resolutely along the wire. In the middle of the river a gust of wind strikes the Singer and the wire, causing both to swing in the breeze. The Singer adjusts for the wind and continues calmly toward the opposite bank. Nearly to the other side, the Singer feels the wire's tension slacken as though it was beginning to pull free of its anchoring. He continues on without fear. The Singer steps off the wire onto the bank just as the wire gives way and falls into the abyss below. Had the Singer ever slowed his progress or lost his focus he would have joined the wire in the abyss.

Reflection

When we are well focused we can easily be oblivious to the dangers that surround us. That can be viewed as either naivete or steadfastness; I prefer the later. When we lose our focus and concentrate on secondary things, we can become fearful, hesitant and stop any forward progress or growth. God does not intend that we play it safe or find the easy way. God has created us for adventure. When our focus is set clearly on that adventure and the purpose for which we have been created, life is full and we are in less danger than when we are preoccupied.

Epiphany 4

Psalm 37:1-11

Do not fret because of the wicked;
  do not be envious of wrongdoers,
for they will soon fade like the grass,
  and wither like the green herb.
Trust in the Lord, and do good;
  so you will live in the land, and enjoy security.
Take delight in the Lord,
  and he will give you the desires of your heart.
Commit your way to the Lord;
  trust in him, and he will act.
He will make your vindication shine like the light,
  and the justice of your cause like the noonday.
Be still before the Lord, and wait patiently for him;
  do not fret over those who prosper in their way,
  over those who carry out evil devices.
Refrain from anger, and forsake wrath.
  Do not fret — it leads only to evil.
For the wicked shall be cut off,
  but those who wait for the Lord shall inherit the land.
Yet a little while, and the wicked will be no more;
  though you look diligently for their place,
  they will not be there.
But the meek shall inherit the land,
  and delight themselves in abundant prosperity.

Alternate Image

The Singer has stumbled on a class of students on a field day. It has been a day they have long looked forward to. However, one of the students is a bully and has squashed a fellow student's lunch. Another has stolen money from a classmate. Some of the joy of the day has gone out of the trip as a result of these activities. Their teacher has invited the Singer to share his thoughts with the class about what has happened. The Singer asks them who lost the most in these acts of unfaithfulness to each other. The students respond that the victims lost most. The Singer asks them to consider the bully; the bully has lost friends and respect of the class, and the thief has to contend with a guilty conscience. Have the bully and the thief not lost the most? The Singer tells them to trust in God completely, to follow the rules that make for happy relationships and their joy will be long lasting.

Reflection

This teaching psalm for students lifts up an important understanding of faithfulness. Faithfulness is placing one's complete trust in God's ultimate justice. That faithfulness is justified, though in the short term it is often difficult to perceive it taking place. We may get all excited about the injustices of the world and their perpetrators and cause ourselves much anguish in the process. This psalm teaches us to think past these short-sighted perceptions to God's intent and plan for the world in which the faithful are indeed the most blessed.

Epiphany 5

Psalm 112:4-9

They rise in the darkness as a light for the upright;
    they are gracious, merciful, and righteous.
It is well with those who deal generously and lend,
    who conduct their affairs with justice.
For the righteous will never be moved;
    they will be remembered forever.
They are not afraid of evil tidings;
    their hearts are firm, secure in the Lord.
Their hearts are steady, they will not be afraid;
    in the end they will look in triumph on their foes.
They have distributed freely, they have given to the poor;
    their righteousness endures forever;
    their horn is exalted in honor.

Alternate Image

The Singer ambles down the path on a bright and sunny day. On the path she encounters another traveler and they fall into step with each other. When the sun stands high overhead they stop by a brook for lunch and to rest. They share food from their knapsacks. It tastes even more sweet because it is shared. Refreshed they resume their travels. Near a village they encounter a number of children begging for money. Each reaches into their purse and takes a handful of change and scatters it among the children. They continue on their way happily and feeling well blessed.

Reflection

There are times when we consider the needs of others who have not received much of the bounty of God's material blessings. Sometimes we like to put qualifications on who truly deserves or merits our charity. Has that beggar really tried to find a job and will the gift make him or her slothful? Or we may like to give to show what wonderful folk we are and expect accolades for our generosity. Behind these thoughts often lies the idea that the materially blessed have found favor in God's eyes, and conversely those not so blessed lack God's favor. This psalm does not reflect that attitude. It lifts up for the faithful the sheer joy of sharing and giving as God has shared and given to us. That gives rise to truly joyous almsgiving.

Epiphany 6

Psalm 119:1-8

Happy are those whose way is blameless,
  who walk in the law of the Lord.
Happy are those who keep his decrees,
  who seek him with their whole heart,
who also do no wrong,
  but walk in his ways.
You have commanded your precepts
  to be kept diligently.
O that my ways may be steadfast
  in keeping your statutes!
Then I shall not be put to shame,
  having my eyes fixed on all your commandments.
I will praise you with an upright heart,
  when I learn your righteous ordinances.
I will observe your statutes;
  do not utterly forsake me.

Alternate Image

The Singer encounters a master teacher. The teacher is a word merchant of the highest caliber. When she speaks, in the Singer's mind's eye she sees images, paths and journeys the teacher's words create. Through the teacher's words the Singer is able to travel to places she could never physically travel. On these mental journeys the Singer learns rules of life she might never have deduced in any other way. These insights enhance her current journey. Through the words of this master teacher the Singer can journey to new lands on the globe and to imaginary lands no one has visited. Truly, the teacher provides the Singer with an incredible journey that in turn inspires new songs for the Singer to share with others.

Reflection

At the root of this great psalm is the phrase, "walk in the law of the Lord." The law, the Torah, gives rules for journeys on this earth and for eternity. Great teachers have the ability to create visions for their students. They create pictures and images that allow students to discover truths for themselves that are intensely personal. Great teachers provide the opportunity for God's revelation to break through. If you reflect on teachers who had great impact upon you, it is unlikely you will recall any particular teaching they gave you. However, you also realize that those teachings have become part of your personal psyche and that is why those teachers are remembered so fondly. In the psalms we find the word pictures of master teachers that still provoke intimate revelations for us today.

Epiphany 7

Psalm 62:5-12

For God alone my soul waits in silence,
   for my hope is from him.
He alone is my rock and my salvation,
   my fortress; I shall not be shaken.
On God rests my deliverance and my honor;
   my mighty rock, my refuge is in God.
Trust in him at all times, O people;
   pour out your heart before him;
   God is a refuge for us. Selah
Those of low estate are but a breath,
   those of high estate are a delusion;
   in the balances they go up;
   they are together lighter than a breath.
Put no confidence in extortion,
   and set no vain hopes on robbery;
   if riches increase, do not set your heart on them.
Once God has spoken; twice have I heard this:
   that power belongs to God,
   and steadfast love belongs to you, O Lord.
For you repay to all according to their work.

Alternate Image

   The Singer enters a small village and goes to a diner for lunch. There she encounters a number of village leaders also having lunch. They appear to resent her presence. She overhears them talking about her. They make caustic comments about her clothing, her hair and her features. They laugh at her as she opens the scripture to read while she has her lunch. Soon they become more abusive and blatant in their degradation of her. A waitress catches her eye and tells her to pay them no attention, that she has been in the community for more than 20 years and they still regard her as an outsider and of low estate. The Singer finishes her lunch, leaves a generous tip for the waitress and blows a kiss toward the tables of her mockers. As she leaves the village she offers a sincere prayer for all the members of that village.

Reflection

Wherever there are people there will be those who mock and belittle others; those who will demean our beliefs, our values and our very selves, just to make themselves seem more important. The psalmist in this passage encourages us to just let those folk have their own problems and not let that affect our beliefs and sense of value. As we bask in God's love we can even love those who belittle people of faith. Our value, rich or poor, leader or follower, is based upon God's love and acceptance of us, not upon the capricious judgments of others. That knowledge enables us to rejoice in God's power.

Epiphany 8

Psalm 119:33-40

Teach me, O Lord, the way of your statutes,
    and I will observe it to the end.
Give me understanding,
    that I may keep your law and observe it with my whole heart.
Lead me in the path of your commandments,
    for I delight in it.
Turn my heart to your decrees,
    and not to selfish gain.
Turn my eyes from looking at vanities;
    give me life in your ways.
Confirm to your servant your promise,
    which is for those who fear you.
Turn away the disgrace that I dread,
    for your ordinances are good.
See, I have longed for your precepts;
    in your righteousness give me life.

Alternate Image

    The Singer has taken a wrong turn, has wandered down various dead end roads and cul de sacs. He is hopelessly lost. Like many males he is loathe to admit it but finally in frustration he asks a passerby for directions. A woman listens to his request, then takes a mirror out of her pocketbook and holds it in front of him. He stares at his reflection in the mirror in confusion, wondering what type of dingbat this is who offers him directions. Suddenly he laughs and grins at the woman holding the mirror. Once he stopped looking at himself in the mirror he realized that there was a path behind him that was exactly the one he needed to travel. Her mirror pointed the correct way. The Singer thanks her, turns and resumes his travel with confidence.

Reflection

There are so many things in life that mislead us on our journey. We are easily seduced by power, riches and glory. All of these stem from our vanity. Our pursuit of selfish gain, our narcissism leads us into paths of oblivion and shallowness and our lives are trivialized. Often when life appears meaningless and glum we involve ourselves in introspection. There is nothing wrong with examining our lives. In fact, it is a good idea, but it is better done from the perspective of looking outward for a purpose beyond ourselves. Otherwise introspection just makes our lives more inconsequential and frustrating. We need to look past our images to around us. In finding their needs and the gifts God has given us to minister and share with them, we find meaning for our own existence.

Last Sunday After Epiphany

Psalm 2:6-11

"I have set my king on Zion, my holy hill."
I will tell of the decree of the Lord:
He said to me, "You are my son;
   today I have begotten you.
Ask of me, and I will make the nations your heritage,
   and the ends of the earth your possession.
You shall break them with a rod of iron,
   and dash them in pieces like a potter's vessel."
Now therefore, O kings, be wise; be warned,
   O rulers of the earth.
Serve the Lord with fear,
   with trembling kiss his feet,
or he will be angry, and you will perish in the way;
   for his wrath is quickly kindled.
Happy are all who take refuge in him.

Alternate Image

The Singer enters a village and in the village square there are people building boxes. One carpenter gazing at detailed blueprints builds a very fundamental box and labels it "Decently and in Order." This builder maintains that God is in this box. Another builder following no blueprints whatsoever pounds pieces of wood together with great enthusiasm and fervor and loudly proclaims that God resides in his box. Another carpenter dressed in fine carpenter gear makes elaborate incantations as she builds her rather ornate box. She proudly announces as she burnishes the gold leaf of her box, that God lives in her box. Another carpenter shuts his eyes and meditatively holds various pieces of wood and with eyes shut announces that God lives in his box. And so it goes, builder after builder makes box after box, each proclaiming that God is captured and lives in their box. In the midst of the clamor a tree falls over and smashes all of their boxes. The Singer murmurs that the tree falling was truly an act of God.

Reflection

How we like to mold God into our own image. We love to tell others how we believe God must act. We delight in developing our theologies about God. In the process we inevitably make God out to seem small — small enough to fit our limited perceptions. When we do this we do a disservice to God and ourselves. When Solomon built his house for God he quickly admitted that it could not possibly contain God nor could anything else he could perceive. Solomon was indeed wise.

Ash Wednesday

Psalm 51:1-12

Have mercy on me, O God, according to your steadfast love;
    according to your abundant mercy blot out my transgressions.
Wash me thoroughly from my iniquity,
    and cleanse me from my sin.
For I know my transgressions,
    and my sin is ever before me.
Against you, you alone, have I sinned,
    and done what is evil in your sight,
so that you are justified in your sentence
    and blameless when you pass judgment.
Indeed, I was born guilty,
    a sinner when my mother conceived me.
You desire truth in the inward being;
    therefore teach me wisdom in my secret heart.
Purge me with hyssop, and I shall be clean;
    wash me, and I shall be whiter than snow.
Let me hear joy and gladness;
    let the bones that you have crushed rejoice.
Hide your face from my sins,
    and blot out all my iniquities.
Create in me a clean heart, O God,
    and put a new and right spirit within me.
Do not cast me away from your presence,
    and do not take your holy spirit from me.
Restore to me the joy of your salvation,
    and sustain in me a willing spirit.

Alternate Image

In the village the Singer stands before a judge. The Singer is charged with murder, rape, incest and sodomy. The Singer is guilty and knows it. The Singer is heinous, odius and monstrous even to himself. He knows he deserves the worst of all punishments. He knows he is evil and perverse. He knows he stands beyond any means to atone for his crimes. There is absolutely nothing the Singer can do to obtain the favor of the judge. His own actions have alienated him from all decent people and from the judge. The Singer has faced himself squarely and finds himself disgusting. The worst punishment the Singer can conceive is to be cut off from the judge and the village. The Singer turns to look at the judge and says unabashedly, "I am guilty! Have mercy upon me though I do not deserve it." The judge turns to the Singer and says, "I find you innocent and pure. I find you as virtuous and guiltless as my newborn baby. And I love you just as much." The Singer is overwhelmed.

Reflection

Where do you draw the line between what is forgivable and what is not forgivable? Most of us find a place where we cannot forgive an action. In the time of the psalmist there were two such crimes: murder and rape, which included incest and sodomy. There was nothing one could do to atone for such crimes. King David had committed such crimes, and with Nathan's help, knew it. But greater than David's crime was God's love, mercy and forgiveness. Greater than all human infidelity is God's faithfulness. It is good for us to remember that when we condemn those around us.

Lent 1

Psalm 130

Out of the depths I cry to you, O Lord.
   Lord, hear my voice!
Let your ears be attentive
   to the voice of my supplications!
If you, O Lord, should mark iniquities,
   Lord, who could stand?
But there is forgiveness with you,
   so that you may be revered.
I wait for the Lord, my soul waits,
   and in his word I hope;
my soul waits for the Lord
   more than those who watch in the morning,
   more than those who watch in the morning.
O Israel, hope in the Lord!
   For with the Lord there is steadfast love,
   and with him is great power to redeem.
It is he who will redeem Israel from all its iniquities.

Alternate Image

   The Singer has traveled to hell. She has plenty of company. They share their stories. One inhabitant speaks of her drug and alcohol addiction that has brought her to these depths. Another tells of his sexual perversions which have delivered him to perdition. Another proclaims her intoxication with power that drove her to sell her soul. Another confides about her desire for beauty and sensual glory. The Singer describes her vanity and selfishness. They all bemoan the condition of the depths of their despair. The others continue the diatribe of woe while the Singer turns her eyes heavenward and asks for forgiveness. Immediately she is whisked away into the kinggom of God.

Reflection

Despair is a common human condition. Invariably our despair is rooted in our sinfulness, our vanity, our *hubris*. We bring about our despair, our alienation from others and God by our self absorption. It feels miserable. It is no different for Christians than it is for others, with this exception. We can ask for rescue and receive it because God is faithful.

Lent 2

Psalm 33:18-22

**Truly the eye of the Lord is on those who fear him,
    on those who hope in his steadfast love,
to deliver their soul from death,
    and to keep them alive in famine.
Our soul waits for the Lord;
    he is our help and shield.
Our heart is glad in him,
    because we trust in his holy name.
Let your steadfast love, O Lord, be upon us,
    even as we hope in you.**

Alternate Image

The Singer lies basking in the sunlight in a meadow. The sun's rays bathe him in light and warmth that seeks the inner recesses of his body, mind and spirit. It is a wonderful feeling. The Singer considers what a blessing it is to be where he is. The Singer thinks, "Is this blessing of sun and warmth and good feelings a result of my faithfulness in following God?" Then out of the corner of his eye the Singer sees a loathsome snake also basking in the warmth of the sunshine. A snake, symbol of temptation and treachery; a snake, a living icon of evil, receiving the same blessing of sunshine as the Singer. A smile forms on the Singer's face as he considers how indiscriminate God is in giving blessings to all members of creation.

Reflection

How we like to judge who should and should not receive God's blessings. We evaluate the faithfulness of ourselves and others as a litmus test of who are worthy recipients of God's favors. We delight when we feel God has rewarded us in our faithfulness and in the punishment of those who do not live up to our expectations. We are appalled and dismayed when we are treated unjustly and when the deceitful achieve success. Caught up in our own opinions of our faithfulness or unfaithfulness we can easily overlook God's universal faithfulness to all of creation.

Lent 3

Psalm 95

O come, let us sing to the Lord;
    let us make a joyful noise to the rock of our salvation!
Let us come into his presence with thanksgiving;
    let us make a joyful noise to him with songs of praise!
For the Lord is a great God,
    and a great King above all gods.
In his hands are the depths of the earth;
    the heights of the mountains are his also.
The sea is his, for he made it,
    and the dry land, which his hands have formed.
O come, let us worship and bow down,
    let us kneel before the Lord, our Maker!
For he is our God,
    and we are the people of his pasture,
    and the sheep of his hand.
O that today you would listen to his voice!
    Do not harden your hearts, as the Meribah,
    as on the day at Massah in the wilderness,
when your ancestors tested me,
    and put me to the proof,
    though they had seen my work.
For forty years I loathed that generation
    and said, "They are a people whose hearts go astray,
    and they do not regard my ways."
Therefore in my anger I swore,
    "They shall not enter my rest."

Alternate Image

The Singer is standing in line for tickets to a concert and a man butts into line ahead of her. She is provoked. She watches the man leave with his tickets and sees a woman running through the lobby bump into him, knock him down and then continue on without a word of apology. He looks provoked. The woman running through the lobby exits and dashes up to a cab, but a man steps in front of her and takes the cab. She appears provoked. Much later they all end up sitting next to each other at the concert. The music is wonderful and at the conductor's promoting they all join their voices together in a marvelous chorus of praise and thanksgiving.

Reflection

Charles Spurgeon referred to this psalm as "The Psalm of Provocation," a psalm of warning. Commonly we think of something that provokes us as something that is irritating, such as someone cutting in line in front of us. Such provocations raise our ire and we want to retaliate against such callousness against ourelves. However, if we think of the possible origin of the word, *vocare,* speaks of call; pro-voke, for a call. When we look beyond our own petty insults we may find a common call that can unite us with others.

Lent 4

Psalm 23

The Lord is my shepherd, I shall not want.
   He makes me lie down in green pastures;
he leads me beside still waters;
   he restores my soul.
He leads me in right paths
   for his name's sake.
Even though I walk through the darkest valley,
   I fear no evil;
for you are with me;
   your rod and your staff —
   they comfort me.
You prepare a table before me
   in the presence of my enemies;
you anoint my head with oil;
   my cup overflows.
Surely goodness and mercy shall follow me
   all the days of my life,
and I shall dwell in the house of the Lord
   my whole life long.

Alternate Image

    The Singer has had a difficult few days and is feeling tired and worn. He looks at an invitation to a party and sighs about having one more obligation. When the Singer arrives he is greeted by name at the door by the host who earnestly inquires about his family. His host then introduces him to a couple with whom he finds immediate rapport. A bit later the host returns and offers to show the Singer and his new friends some art work he thinks they will enjoy. They do so and find several others, with similar tastes, admiring the work. As the host leaves, she turns on some music that enhances conversation and their gazing. Soon their host returns and invites them to her table for supper. The food is sumptuous and bounteous. The Singer notes that even his special dietary needs have been attended to. The foods, the wines, the conversation are marvelous and all enjoy this incredible feast. As he gets ready to leave this wonderful home, his hosts invites him to stay with her forever.

Reflection

The psalm that precedes this one is entirely different in tone. The twenty-second Psalm is an appeal to be delivered from life's troubles and expresses that feeling of forsakenness we all have from time to time. How different this psalm is. God is pictured as the perfect host who provides and guides as a shepherd cares for his flock. Often when we just want to survive with a crust of bread, God offers us an unending banquet.

Lent 5

Psalm 116:1-9

I love the Lord, because he has heard
    my voice and my supplications.
Because he inclined his ear to me,
    therefore I will call on him as long as I live.
The snares of death encompassed me;
    the pangs of Sheol laid hold on me;
    I suffered distress and anguish.
Then I called on the name of the Lord:
    "O Lord, I pray, save my life!"
Gracious is the Lord, and righteous;
    our God is merciful.
The Lord protects the simple;
    when I was brought low, he saved me.
Return, O my soul, to your rest,
    for the Lord has dealt bountifully with you.
For you have delivered my soul from death,
    my eyes from tears,
    my feet from stumbling.
I walk before the Lord
    in the land of the living.

Alternate Image

    The Singer opens a groggy anesthetized eye in the hospital room. Vague images of doctors and nurses, bottles and tubes, machines and gurneys blurredly swim by. Disembodied voices tell her all is well and she will be fine. She dozes off. Later she awakens and become more clear eyed. Her doctor visits her and tells her that the operation was long, lengthy and dangerous, but that she should recover fully. As the word of her recovery spreads, anxious faces give way to radiant smiles of shared well-being. Nurses get her up quickly and aid her in recovering full health. She is surrounded by kind, loving and caring folk all day and throughout the night. Late at night in her darkened hospital room the Singer reflects on all these people and how fortunate she is to have their expertise, care and concern. She closes her eyes and gives thanks to God who provides these people as well as her body.

Reflection

Whenever we face life-threatening illness or events we become so much more aware of how precarious life is and of how little control we have over it. We are thankful for health care givers and to family and friends who are present with us during these times. Their very presence is of tremendous solace to us during those difficult times. More so is the presence of God who creates in us the love that we can share at those moments. The psalmist rightly gives thanks for deliverance to God for passing through these times. Often it is God's agents who lift this up in our own consciousness.

Lent 6 (Passion)

Psalm 31:9-16

Be gracious to me, O Lord, for I am in distress;
    my eye wastes away from grief,
    my soul and body also.
For my life is spent with sorrow,
    and my years with sighing;
my strength fails because of my misery,
    and my bones waste away.
I am the scorn of all my adversaries,
    a horror to my neighbors,
an object of dread to my acquaintances;
    those who see me in the street flee from me.
I have passed out of mind like one who is dead;
    I have become like a broken vessel.
For I hear the whispering of many —
    terror all around! —
as they scheme together against me,
    as they plot to take my life.
But I trust in you, O Lord;
    I say, "You are my God."
My times are in your hand;
    deliver me from the hand of my enemies and persecutors.
Let your face shine upon your servant;
    save me in your steadfast love.

Alternate Image

    The Singer is soaked in fear-induced sweat, his body tangled in twisted sheets. His throat is constricted and his stomach burns and turns. He has awakened from a nightmare. His mind turns from his nighttime tribulation to his daytime travails.

The Singer has cancer. The cancer is located in his throat and in his belly. The throat cancer will end his singing career. He thinks the intestinal cancer and the resulting colostomy will make him repugnant to his friends. Life is hellish and he prays for it to end quickly. As time passes in the hospital the Singer learns how to care for his colostomy and loses his fear of it and is assured by the visits of his friends. Convalescing at home the Singer turns to writing music. Notes flow from his pen in adoration of the God who sustained him during his trials and grants him a still abundant life.

Reflection

Catastrophic illness can knock the props from our lives. What we took for granted can quickly be taken away and our lives thrown into confusion and despair. We can lose hope and imagine no worse fate than what has befallen us. We can even see death and oblivion as preferable to life. In the midst of these times God is always present and faithful to our needs, ready to touch and heal us in unusual ways we may never have considered before. When God moves us from what we expect in terms of health and wholeness we may discover new opportunities of life and living never seen before. When these revelations come, life unfolds in marvelous new ways. These revelations pull expressions of praise from our innermost being.

Lent 6 (Palm Sunday)

Psalm 118:19-29

Open to me the gates of righteousness,
 that I may enter through them and give thanks to the Lord.
This is the gate of the Lord;
 the righteous shall enter through it.
I thank you that you have answered me
 and have become my salvation.
The stone that the builders rejected
 has become the chief cornerstone.
This is the Lord's doing;
 it is marvelous in our eyes.
This is the day that the Lord has made;
 let us rejoice and be glad in it.
Save us, we beseech you, O Lord!
 O Lord, we beseech you, give us success!
Blessed is the one who comes in the name of the Lord.
 We bless you from the house of the Lord.
The Lord is God, and he has given us light.
 Bind the festal procession with branches,
 up to the horns of the altar.
You are my God, and I will give thanks to you;
 you are my God, and I will extol you.
O give thanks to the Lord, for he is good,
 for his steadfast love endures forever.

Alternate Image

 The Singer watches two builders at work. One builder selects beautiful polished granite for his foundation. The sharp edges stand resolute and strong, the polished surfaces glisten in the sunlight. Straight and tall stands the building that rests firmly on the firm granite cornerstones. This building draws wonderful reviews in the local papers.

The second builder uses much different cornerstone material. No one seemed to be quite sure what type of stone it is. It does not have sharp, clean edges. Its surfaces are not polished. It doesn't seem firm at all. In fact, it seems a bit spongy and flexes under the weight of the other stones. As a matter of fact, the stone looks plain ugly. Nevertheless, the second builder builds his building on this strange cornerstone. His building looks quite commonplace. The second builder's building does not even rate a paragraph in the local paper. Later, the Singer comes back to the city of the two buildings as part of a work team after the city had suffered a devastating earthquake. Destruction and sorrow are everywhere. The area the Singer is to work is where he had previously watched the two buildings being built. The beautiful tall structure built upon the polished granite lays in ruins. Its sharp edges cracked, the building lies in shambles around them. The other building, built in the strange stone appears exactly as the Singer has left it. Its spongy cornerstones absorbed the shock of the earthquake and that building stands firm and secure. While working on the other buildings, the Singer hears the occupants of the second building emerge and with songs of thanksgiving and praise, go to work helping others.

Reflection

How easy it is to be seduced by glitter and glitz. What can appear strong and powerful to us may just camouflage the inflexible, rigid and brittle. When we put our faith in human ingenuity and the gods of our own creation, we are vulnerable to shaking foundations. But how our voices can rejoice and be glad when our faith lies in our creator.

Monday Of Holy Week

Psalm 36:5-10

Your steadfast love, O Lord, extends to the heavens,
 your faithfulness to the clouds.
Your righteousness is like the mighty mountains,
 your judgments are like the great deep;
 you save humans and animals alike, O Lord.
How precious is your steadfast love, O God!
 All people may take refuge in the shadow of your wings.
They feast on the abundance of your house,
 and you give them drink from the river of your delights.
For with you is the fountain of life;
 in your light we see light.
O continue your steadfast love to those who know you,
 and your salvation to the upright of heart!

Alternate Image

The Singer joins a group who is to have its picture taken for a church directory. One member who is well known for her great faith and obedient living is called for her sitting. The Singer is seated so that she can see the member's image in the photographer's camera. The photographer arranges the woman for the first shot and then looks into the camera and then looks up quickly with a startled expression. The Singer sees what startled the photographer. Instead of the woman's image in the camera there is an image of a beautiful scene of clouds surrounding a mountain — a beautiful and majestic sight, but not the expected one. The photographer moves the devout woman into a new pose and gazes into the camera once more. This time the lens' image is that of children protected from a violent storm by finding refuge in a cave. The befuddled photographer moves the woman into yet another pose. This time the photographer and the Singer see a meadow scene bathed in brilliant sunlight with a sparkling stream running through, and families playing. Pose after pose is tried but the camera captures only wonderful images of God's creation. Beautiful, but unexpected pictures.

Reflection

People of great faith reflect God's faithfulness. When we look at them and what they do we see not so much those people but the God who uses them so well to accomplish God's will in the world. People of great faith are not as fond of their own images as they are of the images of God, and thus reflect those images. People of great faith reflect God's faithfulness. They truly drink from the river of delights.

Tuesday Of Holy Week

Psalm 71:1-12

In you, O Lord, I take refuge;
> let me never be put to shame.
In your righteousness deliver me and rescue me;
> incline your ear to me and save me.
Be to me a rock of refuge, a strong fortress, to save me,
> for you are my rock and my fortress.
Rescue me, O my God, from the hand of the wicked,
> from the grasp of the unjust and cruel.
For you, O Lord, are my hope,
> my trust, O Lord, from my youth.
Upon you I have learned from my birth;
> it was you who took me from my mother's womb.
My praise is continually of you.
I have been like a portent to many,
> but you are my strong refuge.
My mouth is filled with your praise,
> and with your glory all day long.
Do not cast me off in the time of old age;
> do not forsake me when my strength is spent.
For my enemies speak concerning me,
> and those who watch for my life consult together.
They say, "Pursue and seize that person whom God has forsaken,
> for there is no one to deliver."
O God, do not be far from me;
> O my God, make haste to help me!

Alternate Image

The Singer visits an elderly woman in a nursing home. Though her body is frail, the women's eyes reveal and suggest life, intelligence and vibrancy. She shares with the Singer marvelous stories of her youth and how God has been a continual source of blessings in her life. She tells of the people she has known who taught her portions of God's truth. She tells of her family that loved her in her childhood and the family she created with her husband. She tells of God's blessings that surround her with care and affection yet today. She divulges stories of her work life and the purpose she found in it. Story after story she shares about God's saving love in her life — stories that she treasures. Then she invites the Singer to follow her. She goes from room to room visiting with others in the nursing home. She listens to the concerns and worries and offers encouragement. She offers physical help when she can; to search for a lost item, to fetch a box of Kleenex, to hold a hand. She thanks the staff and encourages them in their work. When the Singer leaves, she feels truly blessed by the presence of the one with whom she sought to minister.

Reflection

Salvation is a more pregnant word than we often realize. We generally think of salvation in relation to what God has done for us. Salvation is more than the promise of eternal life. It is the acknowledgment of all the blessings God bestows upon us throughout our lives. But there is even more to salvation than this. Salvation also means being empowered by God's love to care for others as God has cared for us. In infancy we are largely cared for. Nurtured by that care we mature, we learn to care for others. This is the movement of salvation in our lives. There are definite costs involved in the second aspect of salvation but rewards are found in our partnership with God.

Wednesday Of Holy Week

Psalm 70

Be pleased, O God, to deliver me.
 O Lord, make haste to help me!
Let those be put to shame and confusion
 who seek my life.
Let those be turned back and brought to dishonor
 who desire to hurt me.
Let those who say, "Aha, Aha!"
 turn back because of their shame.
Let all who seek you
 rejoice and be glad in you.
Let those who love your salvation say evermore,
 "God is great!"
But I am poor and needy;
 hasten to me, O God!
You are my help and my deliverer;
 O Lord, do not delay!

Alternate Image

   The Singer attends a funeral of a well-known and much revered friend. His friend was a long time member of a downtown church. When his death was imminent, he asked that those who wanted to give memorials in his memory give them to the memorial fund of his church that he dearly loved. And so the gifts came. One brought a large expensive painting, whose colors clashed with the church's decor. Another gave a golden cross of which the most dominant feature was the plaque on its base telling about the donor. Another brought fans that could be placed in the pews, each boldly lettered and featuring his business. Others brought anonymous gifts of money that could be used as the church officers saw fit. The Singer pondered the significance of these gifts and wondered what his friend thought of them.

Reflection

Memorials are reminders. When we see a memorial gift they often remind us of something. Sometimes those gifts remind us of the giver. At other times the gifts are an intrusion into the ambience of a church and just distract us. Other gifts help us center our thoughts and feelings upon the one who is the source of all gifts. Whose memory do we seek to elevate?

Maundy Thursday

Psalm 89:20-21

I have found my servant David;
  with my holy oil I have anointed him;
my hand shall always remain with him;
  my arm also shall strengthen him.

Psalm 89:24
My faithfulness and steadfast love shall be with him;
and in my name his horn shall be exalted.

Psalm 89:26
He shall cry to me, "You are my Father, my God,
and the Rock of my salvation!"

Alternate Image

   The Singer attends an inaugural gathering. Throngs of important people have gathered with other important people. This is the President's inaugural, everyone wants to see and be seen. The Singer observes one young couple who arrive with a toddler. In the midst of greeting and hand pumping the toddler wanders away unseen. The child meanders through the crowd, spies the President, holds out her arms and hollers, "Daddy!" The President reaches down, picks her up and holds her in his arms as he continues to greet his well wishers.

Reflection

How easily we call God, "Father." How audacious it is for us to express such familiarity with the deity. Even King David did not have the audacity to address God in such a manner, despite what this psalm says. It was Jesus, God's only begotten son that enables us to have such intimacy of address with God. Jesus called God, "Daddy," "Father." And, as Jesus is our elder brother and tells us of God's intimate and passionate love for us, we too call God, "Father."

Good Friday

Psalm 22:1-18

My God, my God, why have you forsaken me?
    Why are you so far from helping me,
    from the words of my groaning?
O my God, I cry by day, but you do not answer; and by night,
    but find no rest.
Yet you are holy,
    enthroned on the praises of Israel.
In you our ancestors trusted;
    they trusted, and you delivered them.
To you they cried, and we were saved;
    in you they trusted, and were not put to shame.
But I am a worm, and not human;
    scorned by others, and despised by the people.
All who see me mock at me;
    they make mouths at me, they shake their heads;
"Commit your cause to the Lord; let him deliver —
    let him rescue the one in whom he delights!"
Yet it was you who took me from the womb;
    you kept me safe on my mother's breast.
On you I was cast from my birth,
    and since my mother bore me you have been my God.
Do not be far from me,
    for trouble is near and there is no one to help.
Many bulls encircle me,
    strong bulls of Bashan surround me;
they open wide their mouths at me,
    like a ravening and roaring lion.
I am poured out like water, and all my bones are out of joint;
    my heart is like wax; it is melted within my breast;
my mouth is dried up like a potsherd,
    and my tongue sticks to my jaws;
    you lay me in the dust of death.

> For dogs are all around me;
>   a company of evildoers encircles me.
> My hands and feet have shriveled;
> I can count all my bones.
> They stare and gloat over me;
> they divide my clothes among themselves,
>   and for my clothing they cast lots.

Alternate Image

The Singer is shopping at a mall. In the middle of the mall is a small boy sobbing, crying and bleating like a lamb. Huge tears are running down his face. The Singer stops to comfort the child, to find out what is the matter. Between sobs the boy tells him he is lost and cannot find his family. The boy tells the Singer that his family must have left him because they do not love him anymore. The Singer holds the boy's hand and tells him that his family still loves him but he is just lost; the boy does not believe him. Finally, the Singer sees an anxious family looking frantically about the mall, he waves to them. They spy the boy at the same time he spies them. They rush together with hugs and kisses. Purveying the joyful reunion the Singer and the other harried mall dwellers feel good.

Reflection

Horses neigh, cows moo, mice squeak, elephants trumpet, snakes hiss, birds tweet, but sheep bleat. A bleat is a mournful whining sound of despair. The bleat bespeaks loneliness and isolation. Sheep are social animals and will bleat pitifully when they are lost. How many times do bleats well up in our breasts? Times when we feel alone and abandoned. Times when we feel lost and unloved. Times when we are surrounded by evil and evildoers. Times when we feel that even God has forsaken us. Despite the intensity of those feelings, deep down inside our very soul, we know we are not abandoned, that God is always there for us even in the midst of the depths of our lives. Others may find us from without, but God finds us from within. Such is the nature of faith.

Easter

Psalm 118:14-24

The Lord is my strength and my might;
    he has become my salvation.
There are glad songs of victory in the tents of the righteous:
    "The right hand of the Lord does valiantly;
the right hand of the Lord is exalted;
    the right hand of the Lord does valiantly."
I shall not die, but I shall live,
    and recount the deeds of the Lord.
The Lord has punished me severely,
    but he did not give me over to death.
Open to me the gates of righteousness,
    that I may enter through them and give thanks to the Lord.
This is the gate of the Lord;
    the righteous shall enter through it.
I thank you that you have answered me
    and have become my salvation.
The stone that the builders rejected
    has become the chief cornerstone.
This is the Lord's doing;
    it is marvelous in our eyes.
This is the day that the Lord has made;
    let us rejoice and be glad in it.

Alternate Image

    The Singer awakens feeling sad. Her nighttime slumber has been filled with memories of the previous day and bad dreams. Her parents have condemned her current lifestyle. Her friends think she is wasting her life and tell her so. Her bank has made errors in her account and ruined her credit rating. Her doctor tells her that her poor eating habits have made her ill. Even her dog bit her when she stooped to pet him. She and others have made her life dismal and she is sad and despondent.

The phone rings. Her mother wishes her a cheery good morning and tells her she and her father are sorry for criticizing her. They respect her adult decisions as to the life she wishes to lead and they just want to support and love her. As she gets off the phone there is a knock at the door. A friend enters and asks if she is available to go with a group of her friends for a picnic in the park. She looks outside and sees a bright and sunny day. She feels well and content. In the mail is a letter from the bank telling her that her accounts have been corrected, her credit rating is triple A and they apologize for any inconvenience they have caused her. As she readies to leave the apartment her dog wags his tail and licks her hand. It is a wonderful day and she is glad for it.

Reflection

Johann Frisch said that "Adam introduced a day of sadness, but another day is made by Christ." How often it happens that outside sources and inside influences seem to conspire to make life sad and we become despondent. How wonderful it is when someone comes along to find our spirits and provide for us the opportunity to have a brighter outlook. The resurrection of Jesus Christ is the moment of our resurrection to abundant life as well. His victory is our victory. His entering the kingdom of God is our entrance pass into the kingdom as well. His conquering of death provides exuberance of life for all of us. Truly, this is the day the Lord has made and we can be glad in it.

Easter Evening

Psalm 150

Praise the Lord! Praise God in his sanctuary;
  praise him in his mighty firmament!
Praise him for his mighty deeds;
  praise him according to his surpassing greatness!
Praise him with trumpet sound;
  praise him with lute and harp!
Praise him with tambourine and dance;
  praise him with strings and pipe!
Praise him with clanging cymbals!
Let everything that breathes praise the Lord!
  Praise the Lord!

Alternate Image

The Singer hears clapping. He wonders why there is clapping and where it comes from. He sees a potter spinning a wonderful pot and he hears more clapping. He moves on and sees children playing a game in an empty lot; again he hears clapping. Wandering on he finds a sidewalk musician; he is the only one listening but he still hears applause. He enters a building and finds an old woman scrubbing floors; the hallways echo with clapping. Upstairs he enters an office where business is taking place at a brisk pace; over or under the din of office machinery he still hears clapping. The Singer leaves the building and the city for a weekend on the farm. As he hears the tractor head for the fields, he hears clapping. At noontime as all gather around the table, again he hears clapping. The Singer is asked to give the blessing. As the others fold their hands a big smile steals across the face of the Singer and he begins to clap. Soon all around the table are clapping with all their might and with incredible joy.

Reflection

Is it inappropriate to clap as a means of grace? Is it proper to clap when choirs sing in a church or after a sermon? Is it a form of applause when we use the skills and talents God gives us to create something that adds to the welfare of all? Clapping is a wonderful affirmation of life. It can affirm our creator, who may well applaud our efforts from the splendid to the mundane. And do we not want to give God praise in all aspects of our life including work, leisure and formal worship?

Easter 2

Psalm 16:5-11

The Lord is my chosen portion and my cup;
 you hold my lot.
The boundary lines have fallen for me in pleasant places;
 I have a goodly heritage.
I bless the Lord who gives me counsel;
 in the night also my heart instructs me.
I keep the Lord always before me;
 because he is at my right hand, I shall not be moved.
Therefore my heart is glad, and my soul rejoices;
 my body also rests secure.
For you do not give me up to Sheol,
 or let your faithful one see the Pit.
You show me the path of life.
 In your presence there is fullness of joy;
 in your right hand are pleasures forevermore.

Alternate Image

The Singer awakens in the middle of the night. She needs to go to the bathroom. On her way to the lavatory she thanks God for her kidneys. Recently she has received a kidney transplant, so each time nature calls, she rejoices in the marvel of her transplant. Each time she uses the bathroom she offers her prayers of thanks to God. She sings, "Therefore my kidneys are glad, and my soul rejoices."

Reflection

The word which is translated as "heart" looks more like the Hebrew word for kidney. Therefore the Singer's line of praise may be quite accurate. Both the heart and the kidneys are vital organs. The early Hebrews may have believed that our conscience resided in our kidneys. In this psalm the writer appears to be a new convert and with all the enthusiasm of a new convert gives thanks to God for all things, including body parts we may not often think about. Years ago in preparation for a weekend spiritual retreat those who would be responsible for the leadership of that retreat met regularly to plan for that event. They thought that common time of prayer would build the team and make them grow closer spiritually. They then had to decide upon a time where each of them, no matter where they were, would pray for the health of that retreat. They selected the times when they went to the bathroom. It turned out to be a very effective time of prayer — strange perhaps, but effective. Faith affects all of us from our intellect to our bowels — for that we give thanks.

Easter 3

Psalm 116:12-19

What shall I return to the Lord
    for all his bounty to me?
I will lift up the cup of salvation
    and call on the name of the Lord,
I will pay my vows to the Lord
    in the presence of all his people.
Precious in the sight of the Lord
    is the death of his faithful ones.
O Lord, I am your servant;
    I am your servant, the child of your serving girl.
    You have loosed my bonds.
I will offer to you a thanksgiving sacrifice
    and will call on the name of the Lord.
I will pay my vows to the Lord
    in the presence of all his people,
in the courts of the house of the Lord,
    in your midst, O Jerusalem.
Praise the Lord!

Alternate Image

    Ambling down a country road the Singer hears a bird singing. He listens and is enthralled. The Singer asks the bird, "What can I give you to thank you for your singing?" The bird replies, "Listen to my song." The Singer continues down the road and spies an apple tree loaded with big red apples. The Singer eats an apple. It is delicious. The Singer asks the tree, "What can I give you to thank you for your wonderful apples?" The tree replies, "Eat and enjoy my apples." The Singer comes to an alfalfa field and lies down for a nap in midst of its sweet aroma. When he wakes he asks the field, "What can I do to thank you for sleeping here?" The alfalfa field replies, "Rest, enjoy and inhale the fragrance of my field." The Singer continues down the road filled with the pleasures of life. The Singer turns his head heavenward and asks, "Lord God, what can I give you to show my thanks for the incredible bounty of this world?" God replies, "Accept and enjoy all that I have provided. All is a free gift to you to be enjoyed. However, now that you ask, you will even be happier if you share by blessings with others, and that will make me happier yet."

Reflection

In a "tit-for-tat world" we worry about giving gifts equal to the ones we receive. It is natural for us to want to give back to God blessings in relation to the blessings we have received. We also know that is impossible. This psalm helps us understand that the proper response to God's gifts is acceptance. We need to just accept cups that run over not because we deserve them but because God wants to share them with us. With that attitude it is appropriate to express our gratitude openly and publicly. We can express that gratitude by clearly announcing our faith in God and by sharing with them the gifts God has given us.

Easter 4

Psalm 23

The Lord is my shepherd, I shall not want.
    He makes me lie down in green pastures;
he leads me beside still waters;
    he restores my soul.
He leads me in right paths
    for his name's sake.
Even though I walk through the darkest valley,
    I fear no evil;
for you are with me;
    your rod and your staff —
    they comfort me.
You prepare a table before me
    in the presence of my enemies;
You anoint my head with oil;
    my cup overflows.
Surely goodness and mercy shall follow me
    all the days of my life,
and I shall dwell in the house of the Lord
    my whole life long.

Alternate Image

    The Singer learns she has leukemia. Though the odds are long against survival, there is the possibility of cure by having a bone marrow transplant. The cure is incredibly difficult and painful. Sixty percent of those undergoing the operation will die, many others will not be cured and will die. The Singer decides to undergo the transplant. Following the operation her skin turns black and the pain is beyond anything she has ever experienced. Her entire alimentary tract from mouth to anus sloughs its tissue. Then there is one point she reaches where she feels that she is being held in God's hands for three days. She survives. She sings of God's grace.

Reflection

The story of the Singer in this case is based upon a real story. It happened to a pastor I met who shared his experience with me. It doutbless has happened to many others. Survival here does not seem the main point, apparently only seven of 21 people do survive. But the story of living grace is there. That is the universal appeal of Psalm 23. In the midst of any life experience God finds us and cradles us in his arms and we lose our fear of death or life.

Easter 5

Psalm 31:1-8

In you, O Lord, I seek refuge;
   do not let me ever be put to shame;
   in your righteousness deliver me.
Incline your ear to me;
   rescue me speedily.
Be a rock of refuge for me,
   a strong fortress to save me.
You are indeed my rock and my fortress;
   for your name's sake lead me and guide me,
Take me out of the net that is hidden for me,
   for you are my refuge.
Into your hands I commit my spirit;
   you have redeemed me, O Lord, faithful God.
You hate those who pay regard to worthless idols,
   but I trust in the Lord.
I will exalt and rejoice in your steadfast love,
   because you have seen my affliction;
   you have taken heed of my adversities,
and have not delivered me into the hand of the enemy;
   you have set my feet in a broad place.

Alternate Image

    The Singer encounters a fellow traveler eager to talk. He says, "I really like your coat. I just love nice clothes. I like traveling with others because they help pass my time more pleasantly. I like traveling but I hate the preparation. I like seeing new things. I like plains and mountains and oceans. Each time I see a new place it is like it was made just for my viewing and my enjoyment. I see you are wearing a cross — you must be a Christian. I am very religious myself. I say my prayers every day. I feel very good when I help someone who isn't as gifted or as wealthy as I. I think I am a very good person . . ."

The Singer seizes a pause in the fellow traveler's conversation and says, "You begin every sentence with 'I,' so I think you bore God to tears. God hates idolatry, including those whose idol is self. God hates you!"

The Singer's fellow traveler's mouth hangs open aghast. He cannot believe the Singer's audacity and condemnation. He moves huffily on his way to find someone who will enjoy his presence as much as he does.

Reflection

It is God's nature to love is it not? God loves all people and accepts them just the way they are, right? God only condemns one's sins but still loves the sinner, correct? But in this psalm it says God hates those who show devotion to idols. There are no disclaimers there; God just hates those folk. These seem to be very contradictory ideas. What we can conclude is that God is always passionate about us. Whether God loves or hates us, God has very strong emotions about us. We can also be sure that God pulls faith from us and turns us from people worthy of hate to a people who are the objects of God's love. Faith is so powerful on both God's part and ours.

Easter 6

Psalm 66:8-20

Bless our God, O peoples,
    let the sound of his praise be heard,
who has kept us among the living,
    and has not let our feet slip.
For you, O God, have tested us;
    you have tried us as silver is tried.
You brought us into the net;
    you laid burdens on our backs;
you let people ride over our heads;
    we went through fire and through water;
    yet you have brought us out to a spacious place.
I will come into your house with burnt offerings;
    I will pay you my vows,
those that my lips uttered
    and my mouth promised when I was in trouble.
I will offer to you burnt offerings of fatlings,
    with the smoke of the sacrifice of rams;
I will make an offering of bulls and goats.
    Selah
Come and hear, all you who fear God,
    and I will tell what he has done for me.
I cried aloud to him,
    and he was extolled with my tongue.
If I had cherished iniquity in my heart,
    the Lord would not have listened.
But truly God has listened;
    he has given heed to the words of my prayer.
Blessed be God,
    because he has not rejected my prayer
    or removed his steadfast love from me.

Alternate Image

The Singer attends a worship service in which her friend's child is to be baptized. At the appropriate moment the pastor invites the parents and their baby to come forward with a leader of the congregation. Words are spoken about the meaning and significance of the act of baptism and about the responsibilities of the parents and the church for upbringing of this child of God. It is a touching, significant moment and the people wait in expectation for the pastor to touch the water, then the child for the moment of baptism. Suddenly the pastor yells, "Fire!" Then pours water on the child's head. The mother and father then raise their wet child above their heads for all to see and the congregation applauds.

Reflection

Fire has long been a symbol of hell — God's absence, where sinners roast over searing fires of torment. But fire has also been a symbol of God's presence as when God spoke to Moses from the burning bush. Fire is a powerful image that tests and tries what the fire encounters. Would it not be appropriate to yell fire at a baptism — to dramatize the powerful presence of God and the tests of life we confront as God's children? The water then could also represent the God with us in all these occasions offering respite and solace and comfort as we face life's trails. And the parents are significant symbols of salvation that together, male and female, they represent the God with us on their child's journey of faith.

Ascension Sunday

Psalm 47

Clap your hands, all you peoples;
    shout to God with loud songs of joy.
For the Lord, the Most High, is awesome,
    a great king over all the earth.
He subdued peoples under us,
    and nations under our feet.
He chose our heritage for us,
    the pride of Jacob whom he loves.
        Selah
God has gone up with a shout,
    the Lord with the sound of a trumpet.
Sing praises to God, sing praises;
    sing praises to our King, sing praises.
For God is the king of all the earth;
    sing praises with a psalm.
God is king over the nations;
    God sits on his holy throne.
The princes of the peoples gather
    as the people of the God of Abraham.
For the shields of the earth belong to God;
    he is highly exalted.

Alternate Image

    The Singer attends a Christmas pageant. Choirs sing Christmas carols, liturgies are read, scripture is proclaimed, candles are lighted, recitations are delivered, but the highlight of the evening is the presentation of the nativity play. Those playing angels are truly cherubic. You can smell the hay as shepherds enter the scene with their sheep. The wise men appear truly astute, keen witted and have the clear vision that only the young seem to possess. Mary and Joseph are a beautiful couple that beam their radiance and joy over those assembled. The baby Jesus coos and draws all attention to his perfection. Lines are delivered, scenery is placed and the play unfolds with near perfection. At the conclusion the audience breaks into sincere and heartfelt applause. It is awesome. The Singer gathers his children who had parts in the play and returns home feeling blessed and renewed.

Reflection

The last part of verse seven of this psalm says, "sing praises with a psalm." It could well be translated, "sing praises with a *play.*" Plays can teach us wonderful truths. They can recall important aspects of our history. They lift up for us facets of our faith that are meaningful to us. Good plays are more than just entertainment. They can refresh and renew our faith memories in marvelous ways.

Easter 7

Psalm 68:1-10

Let God rise up, let his enemies be scattered;
    let those who hate him flee before him.
As smoke is driven away, so drive them away;
    as wax melts before the fire,
    let the wicked perish before God.
But let the righteous be joyful;
    let them exalt before God;
    let them be jubilant with joy.
Sing to God, sing praises to his name;
    lift up a song to him who rides upon the clouds —
    his name is the Lord — be exultant before him.
Fathers of orphans and protector of widows
    is God in his holy habitation.
God gives the desolate a home to live in;
    he leads out the prisoners to prosperity,
    but the rebellious live in a parched land.
O God, when you went out before your people,
    when you marched through the wilderness,
        Selah
the earth quaked, the heavens poured down rain
    at the presence of God, the God of Sinai,
    at the presence of God, the God if Israel.
Rain in abundance, O God, you showered abroad;
    you restored your heritage when it languished;
your flock found a dwelling in it;
    in your goodness, O God, you provided for the needy.

Alternate Image

The Singer falls asleep listening to "The Overture of 1812" on her stereo. Her dreams reflect the music. In her dreams she sees God belching cannonballs from his mouth and hurling angry thunderous epitaphs at earthly sinners. God shakes the mountains, frightening those hiding in its caves. Throughout her dreams the thunder continues to roar, the earth tremors, lightning flashes and God lashes against the inhabitants of the land. The Singer awakens as her puppy licks her hands and face. The trauma of the dream vanishes in an instant.

Reflection

God presents many faces to us. God can be angry and wrathful at one moment and tender and merciful the next, or perhaps all at the same time. God creates the conditions for fierce storms and restorative rains. God is warrior and protector. Our God is a god of abundance, whether it be in blessings or chastisements.

Pentecost

Psalm 104:24-34

O Lord, how manifold are your works!
   In wisdom you have made them all;
   the earth is full of your creatures.
Yonder is the sea, great and wide,
   creeping things innumerable are there,
   living things both small and great.
There go the ships,
   and Leviathan that you formed to sport in it.
These all look to you
   to give them their food in due season;
when you give to them, they gather it up;
   when you open your hand,
      they are filled with good things.
When you hide your face, they are dismayed;
   when you take away their breath, they die
   and return to their dust.
When you send forth your spirit, they are created;
   and you renew the face of the ground.
May the glory of the Lord endure forever;
   may the Lord rejoice in his words —
who looks on the earth and it trembles,
   who touches the mountains and they smoke.
I will sing to the Lord as long as I live;
   I will sing praise to my God while I have being.
May my meditation be pleasing to him,
   for I rejoice in the Lord.

Alternate Image

   The Singer is on an intercontinental flight. He has a window seat and a talkative neighbor on the aisle seat. The neighbor talks about what a marvel the plane is on which they are flying, what an incredible piece of technology and what a tremendous human accomplishment. The Singer smiles and looks out his window at the immense land below the plane — land of desert, rich farm land, stupendous mountains and immense bodies of water. His seatmate speaks about what an amazing age they are proviledged to live in, the technological age, the information age, computers that can do marvels unthought of just a few years ago. Human ingenuity has no limits. The Singer peers out at lands and seas that seem timeless, that existed long before and will exist long after him, terrain that is ever changing and ever the same. The Singer's neighbor continues his litany of the works of human beings and human ingenuity and genius. The Singer turns away from the window and asks his neighbor this question, "Who did all that you talk about come from?" The Singer expects to hear the wrong answer.

Reflection

We truly do live in a marvelous age. However, all ages are quite marvelous as well. We are quick to applaud and lift up our own efforts and to extol our own genius and creativity. Pride in achievement is a good thing — to a point. Pride needs always to be crouched in humility and thankfulness. We did not create the land, the resources, the world from which we can build on and from. We really don't create anything. We merely rearrange things. Also, our ability to creatively rearrange, our minds, our intellect, all are gifts that we only receive. Who do all things come from? God, and only God. Praise God from whom all blessings flow, the works of God are truly manifold.

Trinity Sunday

Psalm 33:1-12

Rejoice in the Lord, O you righteous.
   Praise befits the upright.
Praise the Lord with the lyre;
   make melody to him with the harp of ten strings.
Sing to him a new song;
   play skillfully on the strings, with loud shouts.
For the word of the Lord is upright,
   and all his work is done in faithfulness.
He loves righteousoness and justice;
   the earth is full of the steadfast love of the Lord.
By the word of the Lord the heavens were made,
   and all their host by the breath of his mouth.
He gathered the waters of the sea as in a bottle;
   he put the deeps in storehouses.
Let all the earth fear the Lord;
   let all the inhabitants of the world stand in awe of him.
For he spoke, and it came to be;
   he commanded, and it stood firm.
The Lord brings the counsel of the nations to nothing;
   he frustrates the plans of the peoples.
The counsel of the Lord stands forever,
   the thoughts of his heart to all generations.
Happy is the nation whose God is the Lord,
   the people whom he has chosen as his heritage.

Alternate Image

   The Singer has made plans for a picnic with her friends. She wakes the day of the excursion and sees it is raining. Rethinking her plan she goes into the kitchen to fix breakfast and decides on hearty breakfast of eggs, bacon and orange juice to start her day. The two eggs remaining in the frigerator are broken, probably rotten, she has no bacon and the orange juice has turned sour. After eating two pieces of toast she calls her friends with a new plan. They could visit a new museum that is scheduled to open that day. They all gather at her house, jump in her car and head happily to the museum. However, on the way they find three detours that have to be taken which puts them way behind schedule. Eventually they arrive at the museum and find a large sign on the front door saying that the grand opening has been delayed one week due to a strike. The Singer and her friends crawl back into her car and decide to have lunch at a nearby bistro. They arrive and find it entirely packed with a huge waiting line. Nonplussed, they decide to go to a grocery store, buy food for a picnic and return to the Singer's apartment and have a picnic on her living room floor. They have a wonderful time, listen to inspiring music and carry on a delightful conversation. They conclude that this must be the way they were intended to spend their day.

Reflection

How annoying or even maddening it is to have our plans go awry. From simple outings to vocational decisions. When they don't go as we intend we are inclined to complain mightily. Life is full of upsets and redirections which can upset or dismay us. Some of those changes can be devastating, such as the loss of a loved one during retirement when life plans had been made to travel and enjoy the good life. Other plans are changed for the better but are only appreciated in retrospect. It is good for us in those times of change to reflect that God does indeed have a plan for our world and for each one of us. God's plan, while seemingly inconvenient for us or even painful for us, will win out and the world will be better for it. We do not have to understand that plan or even to accept it. But it is good to accept what happens and trust that God's will will be done.

Proper 4

Psalm 33:12-22

Happy is the nation whose God is the Lord,
    the people whom he has chosen as his heritage.
The Lord looks down from heaven;
    he sees all humankind.
From where he sits enthroned
    he watches all the inhabitants of the earth —
he who fashions the hearts of them all,
    and observes all their deeds.
A king is not saved by his great army;
    a warrior is not delivered by his great strength.
The war horse is a vain hope for victory,
    and by its great might it cannot save.
Truly the eye of the Lord is on those who fear him,
    on those who hope in his steadfast love,
to deliver their soul from death,
    and to keep them alive in famine.
Our soul waits for the Lord;
    he is our help and shield.
Our heart is glad in him,
    because we trust in his holy name.
Let your steadfast love, O Lord, be upon us,
    even as we hope in you.

Alternate Image

The Singer and a companion are on a sight-seeing tour. They begin their trip in the city. The companion complains about the traffic and the people and how he can't wait to get away from the noise, the din and the turmoil. The Singer feels the pulse and energy of the people and is vitalized by their ardor. They arrive at a large canyon. The companion sees a big hole, which is a place where one is in danger of falling. It is a possible refuse dump. The Singer is struck by the enormity of the gorge and by how insignificant the people who travel there seem, how sure-footed the mules are that carry people and the beauty of the panorama.

The Singer and his companion move on to a mountain range. The companion sees cold wintry snow and desolate pine trees. The companion sees the danger of avalanche. The companion thinks how hard it must be to climb such a peak. The Singer's mouth hangs open and thinks, "Truly this is purple majesty." The Singer sees how the creatures of the mountain have adapted and delight in their craggy habitat. The Singer considers how it must feel to climb up such a mass and the thrill one has skiing down its snowy slopes.

The travelers move on to a desert plain. The companion sees its barrenness and lifelessness; the searing sun and arid climate; and complains about the sand blowing into his clothes. The Singer is amazed at the lizards and animals that find life in the area, the ever-changing landscapes as the winds move sand dunes and feels the warmth of the sun warming his body.

Eventually the wanderers return home to the city. The companion falls exhausted into his bed. The Singer's thoughts linger on the day, and the marvels of nature they have seen. The variety of life has made each habitat special and nurturing for them. The wonders of the people whose history is so connected to the land they inhabit. The Singer has had a very good time.

Reflection

How our perceptions of our environment vary. Where one sees abundance and another sees emptiness. Where one is invigorated by a setting, another is enervated. Where one sees beauty, another sees ugliness. Where one sees things, another sees relationships. Godly eyes see far more than godless eyes. How we see fashions our hearts.

Proper 5

Psalm 13

How long, O Lord? Will you forget me forever?
    How long will you hide your face from me?
How long must I bear pain in my soul,
    and have sorrow in my heart all day long?
How long shall my enemy be exalted over me?
Consider and answer me, O Lord my God!
    Give light to my eyes, or I will sleep the sleep of death,
and my enemy will say, "I have prevailed;"
    my foes will rejoice because I am shaken.
But I trusted in your steadfast love;
    my heart shall rejoice in your salvation.
I will sing to the Lord,
    because he has dealt bountifully with me.

Alternate Image

    An aged Singer lies on her bed with tears in her eyes. Her joints throb with the pain of arthritis. She looks at the dust on her furniture that she is too tired to dust. She feels as if her soul itself is dusty with neglect and despair. She thinks of her family tucked away in the suburbs, caught up in the activity of their own lives and giving her nary a thought. Her neighbors are uncaring and unfeeling — they seem to even resent her presence and infirmities. She has been a faithful woman, caring for family and others throughout her life. She kissed and bandaged the cuts of her children when they were small and not so small. She brought her parents into her home when they were her age, which caused conflict in her family, but she felt responsible. She kept her husband in her home as well after he was felled by strokes rather than placing him in a nursing home. She served on the hospital auxiliary and took meals to those who needed them. She did all that and much more. But now it is her turn and where are the helpers? Is God so busy that he could not spare a thought for her? Does God even exist?

There is a knock at the door. The Singer drags her body to the door and answers the knock. A deacon from her church asks if he can come in for a bit. They sit and reminisce about their church and the activities they have shared over the years. They reflect on the many people they have known, loved or disliked. They talk about current programs and the future ministry of the church. The deacon tells her that is one reason why he has called. Would the Singer be willing to serve on a long-range planning committee? She has been suggested because of her knowledge, her faith and her commitment to the church. The Singer happily accepts this new call.

Reflection

It is very easy for us to feel sorry for oureselves. We are quick to speak of our own needs and the ministry that should be given to us. When we are feeling low, neglected and put upon, we even question our faith. We can look at ministry as a give-and-take agreement. If we have given our time, talent and resources to God, then shouldn't we also receive in a like manner? And when we think that way we materialize our faith. But rarely is that the real cause of our frustration. What really makes us feel cared for and important is to be given responsibilities — callings to ministry in service of God. The bounty God gives us is providing us with lives of meaning, meaning found in service to others.

Proper 6

Psalm 46

God is our refuge and strength,
   a very present help in trouble.
Therefore we will not fear, though the earth should change,
   though the mountains shake in the heart of the sea;
though its waters roar and foam,
   though the mountains tremble with its tumult.
      Selah
There is a river whose streams make glad the city of God,
   the holy habitation of the Most High.
God is in the midst of the city; it shall not be moved;
   God will help it when the morning dawns.
The nations are in an uproar, the kingdoms totter;
   he utters his voice, the earth melts.
The Lord of hosts is with us;
   the God of Jacob is our refuge.
      Selah.
Come, behold the works of the Lord;
   see what desolations he has brought on the earth.
He makes wars cease to the end of the earth;
   he breaks the bow, and shatters the spear;
   he burns the shields with fire.
"Be still, and know that I am God!
   I am exalted among the nations,
   I am exalted in the earth."
The Lord of hosts is with us;
   the God of Jacob is our refuge.
      Selah

Alternate Image

The Singer comes upon a spring gushing fresh clean sparkling water. The Singer takes a drink. The water is sweet and refreshing. The Singer drinks more. The water seems to flow through his body, refreshing every cell and every tissue and every organ. The Singer drinks more. The Singer feels totally invigorated. The Singer wonders, "Where does this water come from?" There is no evidence of water about — no streams, no creeks, no rivers, no lakes. Yet here is water bubbling out of the ground. Why? Where is the water's source? What causes it to be so refreshing? The Singer does not know but is most pleased that it exists. He gives thanks for the water.

Reflection

Artesian wells intrigue me. Water flows from the ground unexpectedly. There are numerous streams that flow through our lives that refresh and make us glad. The Hebrews spoke of running water as "living water." Truly our lives are irrigated by such living water. Relationships that create, sustain and make us glad of living. It is fitting that we should give thanks for these waters of life that rush through our own lives giving us strength and refuge.

Proper 7

Psalm 91:1-10

You who live in the shelter of the Most High,
    who abide in the shadows of the Almighty,
will say to the Lord, "My refuge and my fortress;
    my God, in whom I trust."
For he will deliver you from the snare of the fowler
    and from the deadly pestilence;
he will cover you with his pinions,
    under his wings you will find refuge;
    his faithfulness is a shield and buckler.
You will not fear the terror of the night,
    or the arrow that flies by day,
or the pestilence that stalks in darkness,
    or the destruction that wastes at noonday.
A thousand may fall at your side,
    ten thousand at your right hand,
    but it will not come near you.
You will only look with your eyes
    and see the punishment of the wicked.
Because you have made the Lord your refuge,
    the Most High your dwelling place,
no evil shall befall you,
    no scourge come near your tent.

Alternate Image

    The Singer is in a secret room reading a secret book. It is not her room but the room of someone wonderful who allows her to come into and utilize its joys. The book tells her about an invincible, irrevocable, unalterable plan for the world. It is a marvelous plan based upon harmony, creativity and love.

Reading this secret book the Singer is filled with confidence, courage and understanding. Armed with the weapons of hope she leaves the secret room and goes about her daily business with assurance and aplomb. Though she suffers the same thing others do in her daily life, they do not weigh her down as they do others. People remark about her fortitude and strength. Many imitate her but do not really understand where her assurance comes from. She invites those who ask into the secret room to read the secret book.

Reflection

Faith is such a marvelous thing. Faith frees us to embrace life. Faith gives us courage where others are fearful. Faith mobilizes us where others cower from life. Faith makes sense of a world where others see only chaos and futility. Faith enables us to see what is good in the world where others see only what is wrong and vile. The secret of faith is no secret at all but a gift made available to all.

Proper 8

Psalm 17:1-7

Here a just cause, O Lord; attend to my cry;
    give ear to my prayer from lips free of deceit.
From you let my vindication come;
    let your eyes see the right.
If you try my heart, if you visit me by night,
    if you test me, you will find no wickedness in me;
    my mouth does not transgress.
As for what others do, by the word of your lips
    I have avoided the ways of the violent.
My steps have held fast to your paths;
    my feet have not slipped.
I call up on you, for you will answer me,
    O God; incline your ear to me, hear my words.
Wondrously show your steadfast love,
    O savior of those who seek refuge
    from their adversaries at your right hand.

Psalm 17:15
As for me, I shall behold your face in righteousness;
    when I awake I shall be satisfied, beholding your likeness.

Alternate Image

    The Singer is filling out a test form. He studies each question and puts down the correct answer. He has studied well and is confident of his answers. He really doesn't care about the course, but it is a requirement for his degree. He thinks he knows exactly what "hoops" his teacher wants him to jump through and he has jumped. After completing the test the Singer reviews his answers and is even more confident that he answered all questions correctly. He turns in his test paper with a smile of confidence and winks assuredly at the other students.

Later his test paper is returned. Eagerly he looks for the grade. He is dumbfounded — his paper has been marked with an "F" grade. He looks through the exam questions to see what questions he could have possibly missed. Not a single answer is marked wrong. The Singer is flabbergasted. Angrily the Singer marches into his instructor's office to resolve this incredible miscarriage of justice. The Singer demands to know why he received an "F" on his exam rather than an "A" which he obviously deserves. The Singer's instructor smiles at the Singer and tells him, indeed, he has answered all the questions correctly, he fulfilled obvious requirements but that was not what the test was about. What the instructor wanted was interest, commitment to the subject, concern over the theme of the course. Though the Singer answered the questions correctly, he totally misunderstood their purpose. The grade stands. The instructor encourages the Singer to think again about the purpose of the course and to retake it.

Reflection

How do you get to enter the kingdom of God? What test do we have to pass to gain entrance to the pearly gates? What hoops does God ask us to jump through in order to merit salvation? What is wrong with all these questions? How quick we are to charge God with injustice if we think we are being dealt with unjustly and not paid/acknowledged for our correctness. It is easy to turn Christianity into a rulebook religion. We are prone to think that if we just fulfill the ten commandments, God must welcome us into the kingdom. When we do that we miss the point entirely. God asks of us what God gives us — faithfulness, *hesed* as the Hebrew has it. God asks of us not to fulfill requirements but to give our total commitment, to dedicate our entire lives to God. God asks for spirit in tune with God's, not merely rule following.

Proper 9

Psalm 124

If it had not been the Lord who was on our side
— let Israel now say —
if it had not been the Lord who was on our side,
when our enemies attacked us,
then they would have swallowed us up alive,
when their anger was kindled against us;
then the flood would have swept us away,
the torrent would have gone over us;
then over us would have gone the raging waters.
Blessed be the Lord,
who has not given us as prey to their teeth.
We have escaped like a bird from the snare of the fowlers;
the snare is broken, and we have escaped.
Our help is in the name of the Lord,
who made heaven and earth.

Alternate Image

The Singer lays in a coma. Her friends gather around her and bemoan her condition. A once vital and alive human being now lies as though swallowed by an evil monster. Her illness crushes them all. They utter cries of despairing prayer while touching the Singer and holding on to each other.

From within the coma the Singer feels as though her hand is being held by her best friend. She frolics in a field with her friend playing a wonderful game where all the best players have been chosen for her side. Later they all go swimming in a pool of mysterious waters that comfort and make their bodies tingle — all the while she has her buddy with her. It is a wonderful experience.

The Singer awakens from her coma as Jonah was spewed from the whale. The Singer and her friends all rejoice and give thanks for God's presence in all places and at all times.

Reflection

Sometimes we have Jonah experiences. Times when we feel swallowed by adversity and powers beyond our control. At those times we need to remember that God is always with us no matter where we are. That knowledge, that faith, that trust enable us to persevere and even rejoice. We can delight that we always have God with us.

Proper 10

Psalm 69:6-15

Do not let those who hope in you be put to shame because
of me,
O Lord God of hosts;
do not let those who seek you be dishonored because of me,
O God of Israel.
It is for your sake that I have borne reproach,
that shame has covered my face.
I have become a stranger to my kindred,
an alien to my mother's children.
It is zeal for your house that has consumed me;
the insults of those who insult you have fallen on me.
When I humbled my soul with fasting,
they insulted me for doing so.
When I made sackcloth my clothing,
I became a byword to them.
I am the subject of gossip for those who sit in the gate,
and the drunkards make songs about me.
But as for me, my prayer is to you, O Lord.
At an acceptable time, O God,
in the abundance of your steadfast love, answer me.
With your faithful help rescue me
from sinking in the mire;
let me be delivered from my enemies
and from the deep waters.
Do not let the flood sweep over me,
or the deep swallow me up,
or the Pit close its mouth over me.

Alternate Image

The Singer sits down at the bargaining table. "Let me remind you that we do have a contract," he begins. "I know that I have not always lived up to my end of the contract. However, it is in your self-interest that you fulfill the terms of that contract." The Singer continues, "It is well known in our community that we do have a contract. If you do not fulfill your contract with me, what will the others think?" The Singer gathers steam and speaks more forcefully, "If they see a person like me, who has indeed tried to be faithful to our contract and yet is not protected by you, how much less they will trust you and want to have further dealings with you. Truly, it is in your best interest to care for me. If you do not, the drunken skeptics will laugh at both of us."

There is no response from the other end of the bargaining table. The Singer considers that perhaps he has spoken too forcefully. The Singer mulls over their contract. He has everything to gain in that contract. It is a contract that in essence is a gift. Humbly the Singer speaks again, "Let the skeptics laugh, let them scoff and ridicule. I know better. You have always honored our contract, even when I broke it repeatedly. I will continue to trust you implicitly always. In your word I will maintain my trust."

Reflection

Whenever we begin to bargain with God and talk about our "just rewards," we are skating on thin ice. Our contract, our covenant with God is not a contract of equals. In the covenant God merely informs us as to what God will do and what our responsibilities are. The point of the covenant is to give us not what we deserve, but what we do not merit. We are a people gifted. We are a people in a relationship. That is what contracts are about ultimately — relationships. We give thanks to our God of covenants and relationships.

Proper 11

Psalm 103:1-13

Bless the Lord, O my soul,
    and all that is within me, bless his holy name.
Bless the Lord, O my soul,
    and do not forget all his benefits —
who forgives all your iniquity,
    who heals all your diseases,
who redeems your life from the Pit,
    who crowns you with steadfast love and mercy,
who satisfies you with good as long as you live
    so that your youth is renewed like the eagle's.
The Lord works vindication and justice
    for all who are oppressed.
He made known his ways to Moses,
    his acts to the people of Israel.
The Lord is merciful and gracious,
    slow to anger and abounding in steadfast love.
He will not always accuse,
    nor will he keep his anger forever.
He does not deal with us according to our sins,
    nor repay us according to our iniquities.
For as the heavens are high above the earth,
    so great is his steadfast love toward those who fear him;
as far as the east is from the west,
    so far he removes our transgressions from us.
As a father has compassion for his children,
    so the Lord has compassion for those who fear him.

Alternate Image

    The Singer searches for her glasses. She can hardly see a thing without them, so she needs them. She searches high and low in her bedroom, the bathroom, in the kitchen and living room. She looks and looks and looks and finally in despair she runs her hand through her hair and finds them perched atop her head. She laughs at herself and puts them on her nose. Now she can search for what she needed to find with her glasses. She searches for her grocery list. She checks the door of the refrigerator, a logical and reasonable place where she frequently posts her list; it is not there. She looks on her kitchen bulletin board, another reasonable place, but it is not there. She dumps out the contents of her purse and discoveres a multitude of missing items, but not her grocery list. Room after room, drawer after drawer, desk and table, pockets and files, place after places she searches and searches. The grocery list is not to be found. She gives up. In her search, however, she found an address of an old friend she wants to write to and she found a bracelet given to her by her husband on their anniversary. She also found the Bible she had as a youth. A well used Bible then, loaded with underlined passages and notes in the margins. She opens the Bible to a long familiar passage, "He does not deal with us according to our sins, nor repay us according to our iniquities. For as the heavens are high above the earth, so great is his steadfast love toward those who fear him; as far as the east is from the west, so far he removes our transgressions from us." The Singer laughs, "God loses things as well."

Reflection

Though it is often frustrating to lose things, and we are aggravated when we forget things; it can also be a blessing. It is good for us to forget wrongs done us, to overlook a personal slight or dig, to disregard an angry yell, to ignore rudeness. A great part of forgiving is forgetting. How many arguments get pointlessly escalated when we bring up the sins of the past which have nothing to do with the present discussion? It is good at times to be forgetful and to lose memory of past wrongs. God is forgetful. God forgets our sins and removes them so far from his consciousness they are never seen again. What a blessing for us is God's forgetfulness.

Proper 12

Psalm 105:1-11

O give thanks to the Lord, call on his name,
    make known his deeds among the peoples.
Sing to him, sing praises to him;
    tell of all his wonderful works.
Glory in his holy name;
    let the hearts of those who seek the Lord rejoice.
Seek the Lord and his strength;
    seek his presence continually.
Remember the wonderful works he has done, his miracles,
    and the judgments he uttered,
O offspring of his servant Abraham, children of Jacob,
    his chosen ones.
He is the Lord our God;
    his judgments are in all the earth.
He is mindful of his covenant forever,
    of the word that he commanded, for a thousand generations,
the covenant that he made with Abraham,
    his sworn promise to Isaac,
which he confirmed to Jacob as a statute,
    to Israel as an everlasting covenant,
saying, "To you I will give the land of Canaan
    as your portion for an inheritance."

Alternate Image

    The Singer is dead tired. He is burnt out by his work and desperate for relaxation and ease of his stress. The Singer decides to attend a spiritual retreat. On the way there he encounters an accident. He stops, lends what assistance he can, calls for a wrecker and ambulance and when all seems well, he continues on his way to the retreat. Arriving late he enters the retreat ground and is met by a man with tools who hands him a hammer and says he can help a team working on a wall he shows the Singer. The Singer sighs, throws his suitcase on the floor, picks up the hammer and aids in the construction of a new building. Hours later they break for supper. Gladly the Singer walks to the dining room where he is met by another person who shows him where he can stand to ladle out soup to those going through the supper line. The Singer complies and eventually eats his own supper. At the end of the meal hour evening worship is announced. The Singer makes his way to the sanctuary where he is met and asked if he will read the scripture readings and help take up the collection. After the service the Singer heads to the dormitory where he is to stay. On his way he passes a bulletin board that lists tomorrow's activities. His name is all over those pages. "Some relaxation," he sighs. Later, lying on his bed, he realizes that though he is very tired, it is a very good tired. The Singer feels relaxed and satisfied. He has done worthwhile work that has and will benefit others. The Singer feels a sense of accomplishment and satisfaction. He is glad he has come to this "retreat."

Reflection

How often we want to run away from life when it seems burdensome, when we really should be running toward life. Not running toward meaningless activity but meaningful activity that gives us a sense of purpose, accomplishment and belonging. Often we come to God or the church to be nourished, to have our spiritual tanks filled so we may deal with another week. But if we look beyond our personal needs we are more likely to find spiritual refreshment. We are a chosen people, chosen not to be reclusive but to do God's bidding. When we respond to God's will, we are energized by God's spirit and find refreshment in the ordained work. In doing so, we give thanks and sing God's praises.

Proper 13

Psalm 143:1-10

Hear my prayer, O Lord;
  give ear to my supplications in your faithfulness;
  answer me in your righteousness.
Do not enter into judgment with your servant,
  for no one living is righteous before you.
For the enemy has pursued me, crushing my life to the ground,
  making me sit in darkness like those long dead.
Therefore my spirit faints within me;
  my heart within me is appalled.
I remember the days of old, I think about all your deeds,
  I meditate on the works of your hands.
I stretch out my hands to you;
  my soul thirsts for you like a parched land.
    Selah
Answer me quickly, O Lord;
  my spirit fails.
Do not hide your face from me,
  or I shall be like those who go down to the Pit.
Let me hear of your steadfast love in the morning,
  for in you I put my trust.
Teach me the way I should go,
  for to you I lift up my soul.
Save me, O Lord, from my enemies;
  I have fled to you for refuge.
Teach me to do your will,
  for you are my God.
Let your good spirit lead me on a level path.

Alternate Image

The Singer is guilty! She has been charged with a capital crime. She has gone on trial and received judgment. At the beginning of her trial she maintained her innocence, but as the trial went on and the evidence about her life mounted, she changed her plea to guilty. She has been found guilty of a capital crime to where there is only one sentence — death. She has no quarrel with the verdict. Knowing that what she is to receive is justice she marches resolutely to her death. No appeal is filed. She loses her life justly, if with remorse.

The Singer awakens from her nightmare with a start. She is alive, vibrantly alive. It has all been a bad dream, or has it? The review of her life in her dream was accurate. She is guilty. A just verdict would be death. But she stands before a God who moves beyond justice to mercy. A God who is faithful and righteous even if she is not. A God who finds her innocent.

Reflection

The psalmist has no quarrel with a guilty verdict. This is a psalm of true penitence. But the psalmist is cagey and asks God to judge him not with justice but with God's own faithfulness. The psalmist, like all of us deep down inside, knows he is a sinner, that all aspects of our lives are corrupted by our sin. So the psalmist does not ask for justice but for God's love. The psalmist and we receive the verdict — God's love. This love is so powerful we are enabled to love as well. By the expression of that love in our lives we witness to God's faithfulness.

Proper 14

Psalm 106:4-12

Remember me, O Lord, when you show favor to your people;
  help me when you deliver them;
that I may see the prosperity of your chosen ones,
    that I may rejoice in the gladness of your nation,
    that I may glory in your heritage.
Both we and our ancestors have sinned;
    we have committed iniquity, have done wickedly.
Our ancestors, when they were in Egypt,
    did not consider your wonderful works;
    they did not remember the abundance of your steadfast
      love,
    but rebelled against the Most High at the Red Sea.
Yet he saved them for his name's sake,
    so that he might make known his mighty power.
He rebuked the Red Sea, and it became dry;
    he led them through the deep as through a desert.
So he saved them from the hand of the foe,
    and delivered them from the hand of the enemy.
The waters covered their adversaries;
    not one of them was left.
Then they believed his words;
    they sang his praise.

Alternate Image

   The Singer is at a family reunion. Grandpa and grandma, aunts and uncles, fathers and mothers and cousins of all shapes and sizes have come together in celebration of being a family. Memories of past family events are shared and retold over and over again. The best stories always seem to be told by one uncle. When he tells the stories they seem livelier and more interesting than when others tell of the same events. One suspects that this uncle stretches the stories considerably and some may be outright fabrications. But his stories are always interesting. They fascinate young and old alike. They are the stories that bind them all together. They are stories about them. The Singer delights in listening to all the stories and also tells or sings stories himself. Family reunions are wonderful affairs.

Reflection

This psalm is a story psalm. It is a story that brings to life in the telling, important events of Israel's history. The accuracy of the stories is not nearly as important as the telling of the stories, the interpretation of events. In essence, they are family stories. Families are connected by blood, governmental, social and religious relationships. Most importantly, they are stories about God. They are God's stories with God in relationship to this people. They are wonderful stories. They are stories we need to repeat over and over again when the family of God, the brothers and sisters of Jesus Christ, gather together in reunion — reunions of worship, church school and fellowship. They are our family stories.

Proper 15

Psalm 78:1-3

Give ear, O my people, to my teaching;
    incline your ears to the words of my mouth.
I will open my mouth in a parable;
    I will utter dark sayings from of old,
things that we have heard and known,
    that our ancestors have told us.

Psalm 78:10-20

They did not keep God's covenant,
    but refused to walk according to his law.
They forgot what he had done,
    and the miracles that he had shown them.
In the sight of their ancestors
    he worked marvels in the land of Egypt,
    in the fields of Zoan.
He divided the sea and let them pass through it,
    and made the waters stand like a heap.
In the daytime he led them with a cloud,
    and all night long with a fiery light.
He split rocks open in the wilderness,
    and gave them drink abundantly as from the deep.
He made streams come out of the rock,
    and caused waters to flow down like rivers.
Yet they sinned still more against him,
    rebelling against the Most High in the desert.
They tested God in their heart by demanding the food they
    craved.
They spoke against God, saying,
    "Can God spread a table in the wilderness?
Even though he struck the rock
    so that water gushed out and torrents overflowed,
    can he also give bread, or provide meat for his people?"

Alternate Image

The Singer goes with another Singer to a school where her friend is a teacher. They enter the classroom and students quickly gather around her friend. It is obvious that they like her, even love her. The bell rings and the students rush noisily to their seats. Once settled they turn their attention to their teacher. She begins her class by saying, "Listen very carefully to every word I say because what I am going to tell you is very important." Then she turns her back to her class and begins drawing on the blackboard. Beautiful pictures soon fill the blackboard. Pictures that the students recognize and delight over. The blackboard filled, the teacher continues to draw on pieces of newsprint and erasable marker boards all around the room. Before long there are pictures all over every wall in the room. There are wonderful pictures of life. There are pictures of history, geography, sociology, anthropology, music, philosophy and pictures of all types. The bell rings for recess and the students scamper out of the classroom to play. Only at that point does the Singer realize that her friend has not said a single word since she told her class to listen.

Reflection

Do we have the audacity or the courage to tell people to listen to us carefully, because what we have to say is of supreme importance? Do teachers believe what they have to teach is essential for the lives of their students? Do preachers believe they offer God's living word to their congregations? Do parents believe that what they say and do will determine the quality of the life of the offspring? Courage or audacity, it is true. We teach, not just by words, but by the pictures of our lives. We teach with smiles and frowns, with anger and love. We teach in our work and our play, our creations and our recreations. Our teachings are very, very important. Our teachings, verbal or non-verbal, teach our beliefs and values. Our teachings determine the future. Our teachings need always to be based upon our faithfulness to God.

Proper 16

Psalm 95

O come, let us sing to the Lord;
    let us make a joyful noise to the rock of our salvation!
Let us come into his presence with thanksgiving;
    let us make a joyful noise to him with songs of praise!
For the Lord is a great God,
    and a great King above all gods.
In his hand are the depths of the earth;
    the heights of the mountains are his also.
The sea is his, for he made it,
    and the dry land, which his hands have formed.
O come, let us worship and bow down,
    let us kneel before the Lord, our Maker!
For he is our God,
    and we are the people of his pasture,
    and the sheep of his hand.
O that today you would listen to his voice!
    Do not harden your hearts, as at Meribah,
    as on the day at Massah in the wilderness,
when your ancestors tested me,
    and put me to the proof,
    though they had seen my work.
For forty years I loathed that generation
    and said, "They are a people whose hearts go astray,
    and they do not regard my ways."
Therefore in my anger I swore,
    "They shall not enter my rest."

Alternate Image

    The Singer meanders past a picturesque farmstead, warm and inviting. The Singer spies a large sign reading, "Beware of Dog!'' The Singer continues down the road and finds a delightful lawn overflowing with lush green grass that invites toes to wriggle and bodies to recline on its natural mattress. Then the Singer sees another sign. It says, "Keep Off the Grass!" The Singer walks down the road encountering sign after sign: "Don't Walk," "Slow Children Playing," "Yield," "Stop," "No Parking," "Speed Zone," and the like. Impersonal signs telling the Singer what to do and what not to do. The Singer considers, "Do these signs impinge on my personal freedom or enhance it. If I had walked up to the farm house unaware of a vicious dog, I might have been injured. If everyone walked across the grass it would soon become a worn and dusty trail. The traffic signs help me to cooperate with others so that we might all travel safely." The Singer continues down the road enjoying the vivid scenes and carefully reads the signs and follows their instructions.

Reflection

How often we chaff under rules, including God's rules. We see those rules as personal affronts and annoying limitations to our personal freedom. We fail to appreciate that most rules help us to live our lives cooperatively and more fully. Rules help us and God's rules help us to live the abundant life. Consider also how God must feel when we repeatedly break these rules for living. How we must grieve and disgust, even nauseate, our God by our rebelliousness. What may grieve God the most is not that we break God's laws, but that in doing so we alienate ourselves from each other and God. God wants a warm, friendly, cooperative loving family and grieves when that is not the case. God grieves when we pull unrighteous judgment down upon ourselves.

Proper 17

Psalm 114

When Israel went out from Egypt,
    the house of Jacob from a people of strange language,
Judah became God's sanctuary,
    Israel his dominion.
The sea looked and fled;
    Jordan turned back.
The mountains skipped like rams,
    the hills like lambs.
Why is it, O sea, that you flee?
    O Jordan, that you turn back?
O mountains, that you skip like rams?
    O hills, like lambs?
Tremble, O earth, at the presence of the Lord,
    at the presence of the God of Jacob,
who turns the rock into a pool of water,
    the flint into a spring of water.

Alternate Image

    The Singer is in a sanctuary listening to a persuasive preacher. The preacher's words are powerful and moving. They create such forceful and compelling images, it is as though God is present in that building. The Singer notices a small boy next to her squirming in the pew. She wonders, "Does he squirm because the pew is uncomfortable or has God's reality made him uncomfortable?" With that thought in mind, the Singer begins to glance at others in the pews. They, too, give appearances of squirming and fidgeting in their pews. It even seems to the Singer that as her eye surveys the room from the corner of her eye that the pews, the pulpit, the candles, even the physical contents of the sanctuary, also seem to squirm in God's presence. The Singer reaches out her hand and takes the hand of the squirming boy. Together they listen to the preacher, one moment trembling, the next swept up in joy and affirmation.

Reflection

What an amazing short psalm this is. It lifts up the history of God on our planet. It indicates how God's presence makes creation stand in awe of the creator. It is good for us to stand in awe of God. It is good for us to see the hand of God in creation and to be overwhelmed by God's creativity. It is good for us to squirm as we feel God's presence.

Proper 18

Psalm 115:1-11

Not to us, O Lord, not to us, but to your name give glory,
    for the sake of your steadfast love and your faithfulness.
Why should the nations say,
    "Where is their God?"
Our God is in the heavens;
    he does whatever he pleases.
Their idols are silver and gold,
    the work of human hands.
They have mouths, but do not speak;
    eyes, but do not see.
They have ears, but do not hear;
    noses, but do not smell.
They have hands, but do not feel;
    feet, but do not walk;
  they make no sound in their throats.
Those who make them are like them;
    so are all who trust in them.
O Israel, trust in the Lord!
    He is their help and their shield.
O house of Aaron, trust in the Lord!
    He is their help and their shield.
You who fear the Lord, trust in the Lord!
    He is their help and their shield.

Alternate Image

    The Singer attends a dinner of tribute. One of his fellow Singers is being honored by fans and peers. One stands to give the speech of tribute and honor about the Singer's life. The speech maker begins his litany of achievements but somehow manages to talk more about himself than the one being honored. When the speaker tells of the honoree's original songs, he ends up spending more time telling about his own. When he talks about the Singer's vocal achievements, he vocalizes himself. When he talks about the Singer's work for social causes, he tells more about the causes he espouses. When he talks about the Singer's family and friends he depicts himself as the pivotal and most influential person. The speaker's self aggrandizement is so blatant all feel embarrassed. Finally, the speech is over and the Singer who is to be honored is asked to say a few words. The Singer humbly tells those gathered that all honor belongs to God who created him, who gifted him with talents, who enabled him to share those talents with others, and to have a life of meaning. He gives thanks to God for his life. Out of the corner of his eye the Singer spies the original speaker, who is busily talking to one next to him, oblivious to the profound words just uttered.

Reflection

How we love to make tiny gods of ourselves. We love to sing about our own accomplishments. We love to tell of our achievements. We treasure honors and awards that come our way as our just dues. This is idolatry.

How much comfort does a wooden plaque provide? Does it provide any joy to hug a golden or silver trophy? How long can one hear the accolades of a crowd? At best, mementos of achievement trigger our memories of those who celebrated a joy with us, and that is good. At worst, they build our vanity and seduce us into thinking we are godlike.

All praises and honors ultimately belong to God. It is God's faithfulness and love that provides for all that we have. It is God who provides us with security and a sense of meaning and importance — importance based upon being part of God's plan for creation.

Proper 19

Psalm 19:7-14

The law of the Lord is perfect, reviving the soul;
    the decrees of the Lord are sure, making wise the simple;
the precepts of the Lord are right, rejoicing the heart;
    the commandment of the Lord is clear, enlightening the eyes;
the fear of the Lord is pure, enduring forever;
    the ordinances of the Lord are true
    and righteous altogether.
More to be desired are they than gold, even much fine gold;
    sweeter also than honey, and drippings of the honeycomb.
Moreover by them is your servant warned;
    in keeping them there is great reward.
But who can detect their errors?
    Clear me from hidden faults.
Keep back your servant also from the insolent;
    do not let them have dominion over me.
Then I shall be blameless,
    and innocent of great transgression.
Let the words of my mouth
    and the meditation of my heart be acceptable to you, O Lord,
    my rock and my redeemer.

Alternate Image

    The Singer has read a wonderful book. It is a book that has uncanny insights into life. The words in the book practically leap off the page into the reader's mind and heart. The book is full of profound philosophy and practical advice. It is a book to be treasured and used. It is a book that beckons you to share. The Singer goes to the bookstore and buys two new copies of the book. She decides she will share these copies of the book with total strangers. Strangers who she hopes will read and treasure the book as much as she does.

The Singer goes to the city park and watches for possible recipients of her book. Her eyes come to rest on a young man playing with children. He is a shabbily dressed man, but a man who exhibits love and caring for his children. The Singer decides she wants this man to have her book. She goes to the man and holds out the book to him. He stares at her quizzically and then hesitatingly takes the book from her. He turns the pages of her precious book slowly and then more quickly, but without comprehension. He turns to her with questions in his eyes and says, "Muito obridgado." It is apparent he neither speaks or reads English.

The Singer looks for another recipient for her book. She notices a young "tough" in the park. He is loud and abrasive, rude and crude. The Singer wonders if his gruff exterior hides a heart in need, one who would benefit from the wonderful words in her book. She gathers her courage, walks up to the young man and proffers her book to him. He looks at her as if she has lost her senses. "For me?" he mocks, and then swipes the book from her hands. "Thank you for your gift. Sure there isn't anything else you would like to give me?" he asks suggestively and then walks away. She watches him at a distance. He casually glances at the book, laughs with his coarse friends and tosses it in a garbage can.

Reflection

God wishes to be known to us. But do we want to know God? What hinders God's revelation to us? This psalm suggests that God may be hidden from us through no fault of our own. Like the foreign recipient of the Singer's book, we may lack the language or background or setting to hear God's revelation. Or, we like the young hooligan, may refuse to take the time to open ourselves to God's revelation. Our sin stands in the way of the revelation. Fortunately for us, God's love is much stronger than our sin. God's revelation can shine through all barriers that would ward it away. When God's revelation gets through our sin to us, in turn we seek to become acceptable to God and find that God has already made us acceptable.

Proper 20

Psalm 106:7-8

Our ancestors, when they were in Egypt,
    did not consider your wonderful works;
they did not remember the abundance of your steadfast love,
    but rebelled against the Most High at the Red Sea.
Yet he saved them for his name's sake,
    so that he might make known his mighty power.

Psalm 106:19-23

They made a calf at Horeb
    and worshiped a cast image.
They exchanged the glory of God
    for the image of an ox that eats grass.
They forgot God, their Savior,
    who had done great things in Egypt,
wondrous works in the land of Ham,
    and awesome deeds by the Red Sea.
Therefore he said he would destroy them —
    had not Moses, his chosen one,
stood in the breach before him,
    to turn away his wrath from destroying them.

Alternate Image

    The Singer is consumed with envy. One of his friends always seems to come out ahead of him. His competition always seems to win the race. His opponent inevitably writes the better song. His adversary perpetually turns the better phrase. His rival catches the ladies' eyes more quickly. The Singer's challenger always seems to come out ahead and the Singer is jealous. The Singer tries and tries to outdo his competitor without success. He even tries to emulate his opponent but finds that distasteful. It drives the Singer crazy!

One day the Singer's rival comes to him and tells the Singer that he has always been jealous of the Singer. The rival says he has always seen himself as second best when he compares himself to the Singer. He admires the Singer but seems incapable of overcoming the jealous rivalry he feels. The Singer is amazed and shares his feelings. Knowing and respecting each other with new vision they begin to collaborate on common endeavors. The songs and verse they do together are wondrous and wonderful for others to enjoy.

Reflection

Competition inevitably leads to jealousy. The more we strive against each other in combative situations, the more jealous we become. The more individualistic we are, the more embittered we are about the unfairness of life. God created us as a group. God made us a people to work and share together. When we do as God intended, our work is enhanced, or creativity increases and our satisfaction is optimized. We were created to cooperate and when we do, God is glorified.

Proper 21

Psalm 99

The Lord is king; let the peoples tremble!
   He sits enthroned upon the cherubim; let the earth quake!
The Lord is great in Zion;
   he is exalted over all the peoples.
Let them praise your great and awesome name.
   Holy is he!
Mighty King, lover of justice, you have established equity;
   you have executed justice and righteousness in Jacob.
Extol the Lord our God;
   worship at his footstool.
   Holy is he!
Moses and Aaron were among his priests,
   Samuel also was among those who called on his name.
   They cried to the Lord, and he answered them.
He spoke to them in the pillar of cloud;
   they kept his decrees, and the statutes that he gave them.
O Lord our God, you answered them;
   you were a forgiving God to them,
   but an avenger of their wrongdoings.
Extol the Lord our God, and worship at his holy mountain;
   for the Lord our God is holy.

Alternate Image

    The Singer visits Mount Rushmore. She, along with the other visitors, is overwhelmed by this sculpture. It seems as if it is almost holy ground. The granite faces larger than life are inspiring and uplifting. They speak of human accomplishment and genius. The depicted presidents appear Godlike immortalized on the side of the mountain. The Singer examines the sculptures more closely through powerful binoculars. Through the magnification of her field glasses the Singer sees all the imperfections of the sculpture that were hidden before. The ravages of wind, rain and weather have taken their toll. Such close examination peels away the impression of hallowed ground to reveal clever illusions of rock and cement repairs. The Singer then perceives a magnificent cloud descending over the face of the mountain. The cloud holds a transient sculpture of its own. Sky and cloud bring the feeling of holy ground once again, a feeling that remains in the mind and heart of the Singer.

Reflection

This psalm praises God's holiness. We are often tempted to think of ourselves as holy as well, but as when the Singer more closely examined the sculpture on the mountain, under close examination we find we are not holy at all. Faced with God's holiness we are awestruck. We are awestruck by our own shortcomings in contrast with God's completeness. Sculptures and monuments to our own achievements always fall far short of the glory God reveals in nature. Holy ground surrounds us. We must decide whether to observe and recognize the truly holy ground or revel in our own sinful images.

Proper 22

Psalm 81:1-10

Sing aloud to God our strength;
   shout for joy to the God of Jacob.
Raise a song, sound the tambourine,
   the sweet lyre with the harp.
Blow the trumpet at the new moon,
   at the full moon, on our festal day.
For it is a statute for Israel,
   an ordinance of the God of Jacob.
He made it a decree in Joseph,
   when he went out over the land of Eygpt.
I hear a voice I had not known:
   "I relieved your shoulder of the burden;
   your hands are freed from the basket.
In distress you called, and I rescued you;
   I answered you in the secret place of thunder;
   I tested you at the waters of Meribah. Selah
Hear, O my people, while I admonish you;
   O Israel, if you would but listen to me!
There shall be no strange god among you;
   you shall now bow down to a foreign god.
I am the Lord your God,
   who brought you up out of the land of Egypt.
   Open your mouth wide and I will fill it.

Alternate Image

   The Singer watches bird mates feed their young. The nestlings stretch their necks high, their mouths open wide in expectation of a delicious worm. Each parent takes turns searching for fresh worms and then feeding the expectant offspring. The Singer goes to the grocery store where she watches young parents shop with their children with legs protruding from the rear of their shopping carts. The children shout for various types of breakfast foods, soft drinks and candy. Parents console and cajole them as they make their purchases and cash their paychecks at the checkout counter. The Singer wonders if there is much difference between baby birds and children.

Reflection

"Open your mouth wide and I will fill it." Are fledgling birds or children appreciative of the work, planning and sacrifices of their parents to keep their bellies full and their lives content? Probably not, but that does not keep good parents, of the bird or human variety, from their responsibilities. Parents care for their children because that is the parental thing to do. However, it is nice to have your efforts appreciated. As our children grow we expect them to show appreciation and are disappointed when they don't. The same is true for God. God cares for us, fills our open mouths, because that is the God-like thing to do. God cares for us because that is God's nature. At the same time, as we mature, God expects us to show appreciation as well. That is the reason for worship and adoration. We hunger and thirst for righteousness. Worship in a sense if our mealtime grace, acknowledgment by those who appreciate being well fed.

Proper 23

Psalm 135:1-14

Praise the Lord!
    Praise the name of the Lord;
    give praise, O servants of the Lord,
you that stand in the house of the Lord,
    in the courts of the house of our God.
Praise the Lord, for the Lord is good;
    sing to his name, for he is gracious.
For the Lord has chosen Jacob for himself,
    Israel as his own possession.
For I know that the Lord is great;
    our Lord is above all gods.
Whatever the Lord pleases he does,
    in heaven and on earth,
    in the seas and all deeps.
He it is who makes the clouds rise at the end of the earth;
    he makes lightning for the rain
    and brings out the wind from his storehouses.
He it was who struck down the firstborn of Egypt,
    both human beings and animals;
He sent signs and wonders into your midst,
    O Egypt, against Pharaoh and all his servants.
He struck down many nations and killed mighty kings —
Sihon, king of the Amorites,
    and Og, king of Bashan,
    and all the kingdoms of Canaan —
and gave their land as a heritage,
    a heritage to his people Israel.
Your name, O Lord, endures forever,
    your renown, O Lord, throughout all ages.
For the Lord will vindicate his people,
    and have compassion on his servants.

Alternate Image

The Singer has been hired to write a new song for a company. They tell the Singer that they want her to write a light melodic tune that will catch the listener's ear. They want the verses of the song to lift up their various products and tell how conscientious their company is. The Singer begins to work. As she thinks about the song she decides the instructions they have given her are not good. Instead she writes a full score that shows off her great musical talent. She weaves a complicated melody that only a few could appreciate and only accomplished musicians with a wide vocal range could sing. The lyrics she develops are of an abstract prose. They are complicated and surreal but show her brilliance. The Singer works very hard on her composition and then confidently shows it to her employers. They listen attentively and then fire her on the spot.

Reflection

Who do we intend to praise during worship, God or ourselves? We say God, but don't we also seek to show off? Choirs wish to show off their musical talents. Lectors want to show off their interpretive reading skills. Children just plain show off. Preachers seek to impress the congregations with their intellectual prowess and dramatic flair. Worshipers show off their presence and piety. Who do we think we are impressing? Our vision is often horizontal rather than vertical. This tends to please us. This psalm tells us that God does what God wants to do. We in turn do what God wants us to do. It pleases God to love us. In turn, it should please us to love God and to show that pleasure in praising God alone.

Proper 24

Psalm 146

Praise the Lord!
Praise the Lord, O my soul!
I will praise the Lord as long as I live;
    I will sing praises to my God all my life long.
Do not put your trust in princes,
    in mortals, in whom there is no help.
When their breath departs, they return to the earth;
    on that very day their plans perish.
Happy are those whose help is the God of Jacob,
    whose hope is in the Lord their God,
who made heaven and earth, the sea, and all that is in them;
    who keeps faith forever;
who executes justice for the oppressed;
    who gives food to the hungry.
The Lord sets the prisoners free;
    the Lord opens the eyes of the blind.
The Lord lifts up those who are bowed down;
    the Lord loves the righteous.
The Lord watches over the strangers;
    he upholds the orphan and the widow,
    but the way of the wicked he brings to ruin.
The Lord will reign forever,
    your God, O Zion, for all generations.
Praise the Lord!

Alternate Image

    The Singer's friend has good intentions. His friend asks the Singer to help him write a list of good things he can do with his estate. His friend has accumulated a good deal of wealth and is heir to a great deal more wealth. His friend wants to do things that are important and helpful with all this wealth during his life and following. Each day the Singer and his friend get together and deliberate on good things to do. They consider homeless and hungry children that could be helped. They talk about environmental issues that need to be addressed. They think of scholarships that would enable young people to reach their potential. They consider churches they have belonged to and how their ministries could be aided with more money in their budgets. Day after day they work on their list of good things to do. Finally, the list is complete and they make plans for the friend's lawyer to come and draw up papers of the foundation that will bring all these plans into being. On the way to the lawyer's office the Singer's friend suffers a heart attack and dies.

Reflection

The mid-point of scripture is the third verse of this psalm. It warns us not to place our hope in "princes;" mortals like us for our well being. Despite our good intentions, our plans can and often do go awry. The good we intend can be thwarted by factors we have not considered or by our own sinfulness not fully understood. While it is good to have good feelings for our fellow human beings and it is good to plan, ultimately the only one we can truly trust is God, who is eternal.

Proper 25

Psalm 128

Happy is everyone who fears the Lord,
    who walks in his ways.
You shall eat the fruit of the labor of your hands;
    you shall be happy, and it shall go well with you.
Your wife will be like a fruitful vine within your house;
    your children will be like olive shoots around your table.
Thus shall the man be blessed who fears the Lord.
The Lord bless you from Zion.
    May you see the prosperity of Jerusalem
    all the days of your life.
May you see your children's children.
    Peace be upon Israel!

Alternate Image

    The Singer attends her family's Thanksgiving gathering. Aunts and uncles, cousins and siblings all gather for this festivity. At each end of the great table her grandparents are seated. The conversation around the table is animated and joyous. Stories of fulfilling work, of healthy energetic children, of joys shared and sorrows endured abound at the table. The Singer's family truly enjoys each other and they demonstrate that affection openly with hugs and kisses and stories. Joy abounds and platters of turkey, dressing, cranberry sauce, salads and vegetables are passed. The Singer watches her grandparents during the meal — they positively beam with delight over their family. At the end of the meal as at the beginning, her grandfather offers a heartfelt prayer of thanksgiving.

Reflection

"Thus shall the man be blessed who fears the Lord." This psalm lifts up a truly happy family. Verse four could also be translated this way, "The Reliable One will bless him as a reliable man, because he fears the Lord." Reliability is an essential component of a happy family. Families that can rely on each other are trusting and maintain hope, for that has been their experience. Families that are reliable are strong families. How good it feels to be regarded as a reliable person, a faithful person. Reliability carries a double blessing — the blessing of being well regarded by others and the blessing of feeling good about oneself. Reliability is a great heritage to share with your offspring.

Proper 26

Psalm 127

Unless the Lord builds the house,
  those who build it labor in vain.
Unless the Lord guards the city,
  the guard keeps watch in vain.
It is in vain that you rise up early and go late to rest,
  eating the bread of anxious toil;
  for he gives sleep to his beloved.
Sons are indeed a heritage from the Lord,
  the fruit of the womb a reward.
Like arrows in the hand of a warrior are the sons of one's youth.
  Happy is the man who has
  his quiver full of them.
He shall not be put to shame
  when he speaks with his enemies in the gate.

Alternate Image

The Singer stands before a dilapidated church, with an old man staring forlornly at the decaying ediface. The old man tells the Singer of days gone by when the church was strong and vibrant and beautiful. The man reminisces about the activity and fellowship that the church once had. However, most of the people have gone, leaving only a small remnant who cannot maintain the building or its ministry. The man tells the Singer that their children have either moved away or just don't participate. He bemoans the fact that they just don't seem to care about anyone but themselves. The old man also acknowledges that he and his peers likely trained their children to be exactly the way they are. They taught them the importance of making money, even at the expense of others. They trained them to make a good appearance even if their hearts were not in it. They taught them the importance of things but not relationships. And now their children have wonderful homes and cars and full bank accounts but the church lies empty. They don't even seem to know what they are missing.

Reflection

A sad fact today is that many churches find their numbers decreasing. Children of churchgoers of the past no longer attend church. Materialistic values appear to outweigh spiritual values and the churches diminish. Does this surprise us? From where did the value of materialism and secularism issue if not from ourselves? Thinking of the achievements of the past we often worship at the altar of our own vanity. As we applaud our own efforts and accomplishments we destroy the cornerstones of that which allowed us true security. How better it is to tell our children of the gifts we have received and the faithfulness of God's rather than of our own exploits? When that happens the Lord's house remains strong.

Proper 27

Psalm 50:7-15

"Hear, O my people, and I will speak,
   O Israel, I will testify against you. I am God, your God.
Not for your sacrifices do I rebuke you;
   your burnt offerings are continually before me.
I will not accept a bull from your house,
   or goats from your folds.
For every wild animal of the forest is mine,
   the cattle on a thousand hills.
I know all the birds of the air,
   and all that moves in the field is mine.
If I were hungry, I would not tell you,
   for the world and all that is in it is mine.
Do I eat the flesh of bulls,
   or drink the blood of goats?
Offer to God a sacrifice of thanksgiving,
   and pay your vows to the Most High.
Call on me in the day of trouble;
   I will deliver you, and you shall glorify me."

Alternate Image

    The Singer accompanies a friend of hers who is going home to visit her parents. As they enter her parents' yard her friend picks some flowers from a flower bed. They knock at the door and are welcomed and her friend gives her mother the flowers she has picked. They are shown to her friend's old room to put down the suitcases and to freshen up. Once in the room the Singer's friend rummages through drawers and finds a scarf of her mother's. She places the scarf in a box and they go down for supper. At the table her friend gives the box containing the scarf to her mother. They have a wonderful lunch. During lunch the Singer's friend asks her parents if they still like pizza and upon hearing the affirmative she offers to provide pizza for their supper that evening. After lunch the friend rummages through more drawers and wraps more presents of items her parents already own. Later she calls a pizza parlor and orders pizza for that evening and charges it to her parents. The pizza is burned and the atmosphere is strained as the parents open their presents. The Singer finds the whole occasion very embarrassing but her friend seems oblivious to her own actions. As they leave, her friend bids her parents farewell and they nod with forced smiles. The Singer warmly thanks her friend's parents for their hospitality and care. The parents grab and hug the Singer warmly and invite her back anytime.

Reflection

When we offer God our leftovers how do we think God reacts? When we place our loose change in the collection plate or the salvation army's pots, do we expect accolades? When we carefully make contributions based upon tax advantages, how we can exploit our generosity publicly? Who do we seek to impress? If we give gifts to a church or civic organization do we demand that a large plaque or engraving accompany that gift? Are we extremely affronted when our gifts are not acknowledged in a manner we think is fitting? The psalmist clearly states that God is not impressed with this type of behavior. What we often expect accolades for in relation to our generosity is merely a small portion of the gifts that God has already given us. Perhaps we should be the ones saying thank you when we share our affluence with others.

Proper 28

Psalm 76

In Judah God is known,
 his name is great in Israel.
His abode has been established in Salem,
 his dwelling place in Zion.
There he broke the flashing arrows,
 the shield, the sword, and the weapons of war. Selah
Glorious are you,
 more majestic than the everlasting mountains.
The stouthearted were stripped of their spoil;
 they sank into sleep;
 none of the troops was able to lift a hand.
At your rebuke, O God of Jacob,
 both rider and horse lay stunned.
But you indeed are awesome!
 Who can stand before you when once your anger is roused?
From the heavens you uttered judgment;
 the earth feared and was still
when God rose up to establish judgment,
 to save all the oppressed of the earth. Selah
Human wrath serves only to praise you,
 when you bind the last bit of your wrath around you.
Make vows to the Lord your God, and perform them;
 let all who are around him bring gifts
 to the one who is awesome,
who cuts off the spirit of princes,
 who inspires fear in the kings of the earth.

Alternate Image

 The Singer sits with a friend who has been stricken with cancer. His friend bemoans his fate. He protests the unfairness of his illness, he who has always cared for his body. He speaks about those who abuse their bodies and yet remain healthy — it does not seem fair to him. He complains that his own family has not shown him the proper concern or care, that he has had to bear this burden by himself. He rebuffs the Singer's attempt to talk of God's love in the midst of difficulty with the words, "If God really cared, cancer would not exist and I wouldn't have it."

The Singer visits another friend who had the same cancer at first. This friend tells of the expertise and compassion of his doctors, of the great strides that have been made in cancer research and of the hope he has for himself and others. He tells of how his family has supported him and how he has tried to communicate clearly with them his feelings about himself and about them. He speaks about a support group that he belongs to and how they have helped him cope with his illness. When he hears of the Singer's other friend he offers to go and visit with him and just be there for him if he can. The Singer feels blessed just by being in his friend's presence.

Reflection

There are enemies in the world. Enemies who would separate us from each other either through acts of violence or inattention. There are enemies who would destroy our faith and turn us into cynics. There are enemies who entice us into complete self-absorption and vain lives. These are God's enemies as well. We are God's. We exist because of God. Our life has meaning because of God. Our lives are the arena where God often operates in this world. All of life is an opportunity for us to show our appreciation and thankfulness to the God of our being.

Proper 29

Psalm 23

The Lord is my shepherd, I shall not want.
    He makes me lie down in green pastures;
he leads me beside still waters;
    he restores my soul.
He leads me in right paths
    for his name's sake.
Even though I walk through the darkest valley,
    I fear no evil;
for you are with me;
    your rod and your staff —
    they comfort me.
You prepare a table before me
    in the presence of my enemies;
you anoint my head with oil;
    my cup overflows.
Surely goodness and mercy shall follow me
    all the days of my life,
and I shall dwell in the house of the Lord
    my whole life long.

Alternate Image

    The Singer has been invited to create and sing one of her songs before a large assemblage of other Singers and composers. It is quite an honor. It is also quite frightening. Will she sing on key? Will her music be lyrical and pleasing to their critical ears? Will her voice be strong and clear or will she croak like a frog? Will her lyrics be meaningful or sound like sophomoric gibberish? Will she fall flat on her face as she walks out on stage? Doubts and fears wash over her like flood waters on a sandy beach.

The Singer stops and prays. She hears a voice ask, "Why do you sing? Why do you write songs? What is your purpose in life? The Singer smiles and considers that the gifts she has been given are for sharing with others, otherwise she would not have them. Her talent is a gift for which she is the caretaker. The purpose of her life is to witness to the One who gave her these gifts and stories to share.

The night of the performance the Singer strides confidently on stage and delivers her story in song confidently. She sings faithfully to give God glory. It is a good opportunity for which she gives thanks.

Reflection

We can find the source of confidence sometimes by examining our fears. We can play "what if" games to confront our fears. What if our worst fears came true? Would that destroy our lives? Would we disappear and lose all meaning from our lives? Would we lose our very being? When we follow through on the implications of our fears we find them not nearly as scary as we first imagine. Indeed when we look at ultimate issues we are secure. We are secure because the God who created us, who gave us life, is always present in our lives even into life eternal. That is security. More so, our lives have meaning and purpose because God makes that an integral part of our lives. We have confidence, not because of our own intrinsic abilities, but because of God's power that resides in us. God's faithfulness gives us confidence to do all that God offers us the opportunity to do.

Thanksgiving

Psalm 65

Praise is due to you,
    O God, in Zion;
and to you shall vows be performed,
    O you who answer prayer!
To you all flesh shall come.
When deeds of iniquity overwhelm us,
    you forgive our transgressions.
Happy are those whom you choose and bring near
    to live in your courts.
We shall be satisfied with the goodness of your house,
    your holy temple.
By awesome deeds you answer us with deliverance,
    O God of our salvation;
you are the hope of all the ends of the earth
    and of the farthest seas.
By your strength you established the mountains;
    you are girded with might.
You silence the roaring of the seas,
    the roaring of their waves,
    the tumult of the peoples.
Those who live at earth's farthest bounds are awed by your signs;
you make the gateways of the morning and the evening
    shout for joy.
You visit the earth and water it,
    you greatly enrich it;
the river of God is full of water;
    you provide the people with grain,
    for so you have prepared it.
You water its furrows abundantly,
    settling its ridges,
softening it with showers,
    and blessing its growth.

You crown the year with your bounty;
  your wagon tracks overflow with richness.
The pastures of the wilderness overflow,
  the hills gird themselves with joy,
the meadows clothe themselves with flocks,
  the valleys deck themselves with grain,
  they shout and sing for joy.

Alternate Image

The Singer attends a grape-stomping festival. He wanders down the lane between grape arbors to where a large crowd has gathered around enormous vats. Wagons laden with freshly picked grapes roll in, the last of all the harvest. With shiny pitchforks the grapes are lifted and thrown in to the large round vats. Then the great fun begins. Those gathered around the vats throw themselves into the vats and begin jumping up and down, stomping on the grapes with great enthusiasm. Men and women and children all leap about in the vats with the grape juices squishing between their toes. People of all ages and all sizes hop and prance about in the vats, singing songs of joy and thanksgiving. It has been a wonderful harvest, the people are joyful and happy. All are restored by the fruit of the land.

Reflection

This is a harvest festival psalm. For eight days in September, folks would gather and celebrate the harvest and their freedom. The grape harvest was the last of the harvests for the year. It signaled a time to celebrate what the land had produced and a time to begin work to prepare the land to produce again. Harvest celebrations remind us of the cycle of life. We, as the grain which springs from the ground year after year and is planted for future harvests, are continually renewed by the God who created us. Harvest celebrations remind us of our continuing recreation. It is good for us to celebrate and give thanks on regular and special occasions. It is good for us to gather in groups for celebrations of God's goodness, to shout and sing for joy.

www.ingramcontent.com/pod-product-compliance
Lightning Source LLC
Chambersburg PA
CBHW071725090426

42738CB00009B/1877